W9-AVY-904

gone canoeing

gone canoeing

Weekend Wilderness Adventures in Southern Ontario

Kevin Callan

The BOSTON
MILLS PRESS

When one finally arrives at the point where schedules are forgotten, and
all becomes immersed in ancient rhythms, one begins to live.

Sigurd F. Olson

CANADIAN CATALOGUING
IN PUBLICATION DATA

Callan, Kevin
Gone canoeing : weekend wilderness
adventures in Southern Ontario

Includes bibliographical references.
ISBN 1-55046-326-8

1. Canoes and canoeing – Ontario,
Southern – Guidebooks. 2. Ontario,
Southern – Guidebooks. I. Title.

GV776.15.O5C3443 2001
797.1'22'09713   C00-933201-4

Copyright © 2001 Kevin Callan

05 04 03 02 01   1 2 3 4 5

Published in 2001 by
BOSTON MILLS PRESS
132 Main Street
Erin, Ontario N0B 1T0
Tel 519-833-2407
Fax 519-833-2195
e-mail books@bostonmillspress.com
www.bostonmillspress.com

An affiliate of
STODDART PUBLISHING
CO. LIMITED
895 Don Mills Road
#400 2 Park Centre

Toronto, Ontario
Canada M3C 1W3
Tel 416-445-3333
Fax 416-445-5967
e-mail gdsinc@genpub.com

Distributed in Canada by
GENERAL DISTRIBUTION
SERVICES LIMITED
325 Humber College Boulevard
Toronto, Canada M9W 7C3
Orders 1-800-387-0141 Ontario & Quebec
Orders 1-800-387-0172 NW Ontario
  & other provinces
e-mail customer.service@genpub.com

Distributed in the United States by
GENERAL DISTRIBUTION
SERVICES INC.
PMB 128, 4500 Witmer Industrial Estates
Niagara Falls, New York 14305-1386
Toll-free 1-800-805-1083
Toll-free fax 1-800-481-6207
e-mail gdsinc@genpub.com
www.genpub.com

Design by Mary Firth
Maps by Tim Wykes
Printed in Canada

Photo, page 1: *Face in a cedar tree,*
Beaver River
Photo, page 3: *Long Point's Big Creek*

The Canada Council | Le Conseil des Arts
FOR THE ARTS | DU CANADA
SINCE 1957 | DEPUIS 1957

We acknowledge for their financial support of our publishing program the
Canada Council, the Ontario Arts Council, and the Government of Canada
through the Book Publishing Industry Development Program (BPIDP).

Contents

Acknowledgments

Writing this book would have been impossible without the help of many people. I would first like to thank my canoe companions who shared all those soggy portages, bug-infested campsites and dried-up riverbeds with me during the past two years: brother-in-law Jim Harkin and his sons Ryan and Keelan; brother-in-law Terry Fritzley, son Todd, and his friend Joel; all the canoeheads from the Durham Outdoor Club who joined me and my wife on the Beaver River (don't give up your singing career, Melissa); Doug, Kim, David and Steven Galloway; Hugh Banks and his son Jeremy; Brian McFadzen; Darlene Craig, son Ryan, fiancé Trevor McIlmoyle, and Ryan's friend Jason; Walker "Bass Master" Hudson, his sister Marin and dad, Noel; my dog, Bailey; and especially my wife, Alana, who really is the best canoe partner ever.

Special thanks also to Tim Wykes for producing all the incredible maps (you're a true artist, Tim); the entire gang at Boston Mills Press, especially editor Kathy Fraser; designer Mary Firth; the gang at Wildrock Outfitters for their enthusiasm for each and every project I have done; the staff at Trent Photographics and B&B Outfitters for their expertise; Jim Stevens at Eureka; Bill at Ostrom Packs; Don Otey from Dagger; Peterborough's Angevaare Mazda; Jeff Solway of Nashwaak Paddles; Glenn Fallis of Voyageur Canoe; and Earley Enterprise (builders of the Tripper's Delight Canoe Cart), for supplying me with some great gear throughout this and other book projects.

Finally, I would like to thank my family for all the support they have given me throughout the years, especially my father, who, even after being dumped out of the canoe on our latest fishing trip, still approves of my love for the craft — though he continues to insist that the motorboat is a superior mode of transport for wilderness travel.

Preface

I believe all canoeists dream of that far-off northern canoe route, one that would take at least a month to complete and be free of any roads or cottage development along the way. It would be a place where cell phones wouldn't ring, long grueling portages would be the norm, and the only signs of civilization would be the sound of a jet flying high overhead or the blinking of a satellite spotted among the millions of stars spread out across the night sky.

This guidebook has little to do with such an intense journey. *Gone Canoeing: Weekend Wilderness Adventures in Southern Ontario* is for those moments in between. It's for times when your job limits you to just a lousy weekend to head off and reenergize yourself, for parents looking for a not-so-wild place to introduce their children to the wonders of canoe travel, for when your skill level isn't quite up to snuff yet to take on that extended trip to the north. And it's also for all those lucky paddlers who somehow do find the time to paddle in wild, remote places for long periods of time and are just looking for a quick fix for now while they wait for the ice to thaw.

To canoe these semi-wild routes, you still have to be prepared, however. On Crotch Lake, a place free of any portages, it's important to have a canoe large enough to haul all the cozy lawn chairs, coolers and other campsite paraphernalia you want to make your night out as comfortable as possible. Be sure to bring enough change to purchase a coffee at the park store that's strategically placed halfway along the portage at Murphys Point Provincial Park. And when you meet the fly-in fishermen on Noganosh Lake, the guys who have spent a fortune to "get away from it all," don't forget to be courteous enough to lie about how easy and cheap it was for you simply to paddle in.

Naptime for Jeremy on Pooh Lake.

Alana takes it all in (Noganosh Lake).

When traveling routes that are close to home, what's most important to pack along is a sense of humor. Add cows to your list of possible wildlife sightings while on the Beaver River in Grey County. Before camping at Sauble Falls Provincial Park, it's a good idea to purchase a can of pepper spray to ward off the thieving raccoons that sneak into camp at night. Helmets should be worn on London's Thames River to protect yourself against out-of-control golf balls. And last but certainly not least, irate landowners who, for some reason or another, seem to think they own the rights to the Credit River near Georgetown should be ignored at all cost. Sounds serious, I know, but you should have to deal with a few annoyances in the south before embarking on your dream trip to the far north.

I hope this book inspires you to get your feet wet. Go canoeing!

Big Creek

Long Point has always been a haven for bird watchers, especially during peak migration, when a total of 320 species of birds are known to fly through the area. To help observe this natural occurrence, Long Point Provincial Park and the Canadian Wildlife Service have established a number of prime walking trails through extensive marshland and neighboring sand dunes. Another often overlooked way for birders to search for that rare yellow-headed blackbird or uncommon tufted titmouse is by way of canoe, and Big Creek, the largest navigable stream in the district, is the perfect route choice.

For the past couple of years, the Long Point Conservation Authority has been working on plans to maintain a two-day route on Big Creek from the town of Delhi to its mouth at Long Point's Inner Bay. In recent years, countless logjams have blocked the waterway, making canoeing slow if not impossible, and private land disputes have made access to camping very limited. Even if the conservation authority does manage to continually maintain the entire route, I think I would rather make Long Point Provincial Park my base camp, and then head out on a series of daytrips, using the frequent side-road bridges as put-ins and take-outs. The best of these is a three-to-four-hour paddle between Concession Road 3 and Cronmillar's Marina along Regional Road 59. (An alternative take-out can be had on the northeast side of the Regional Road 42, just before the town of Port Royal.) To access Big Creek, drive 3.5 kilometers west off Regional Road 59 to the Concession Road 3 bridge. Here, park on the southwest side of the bridge and walk down a gated road leading into Rowan Mills Conservation Area. The route's

Facing page: Big Creek meanders through a jungle-like landscape.

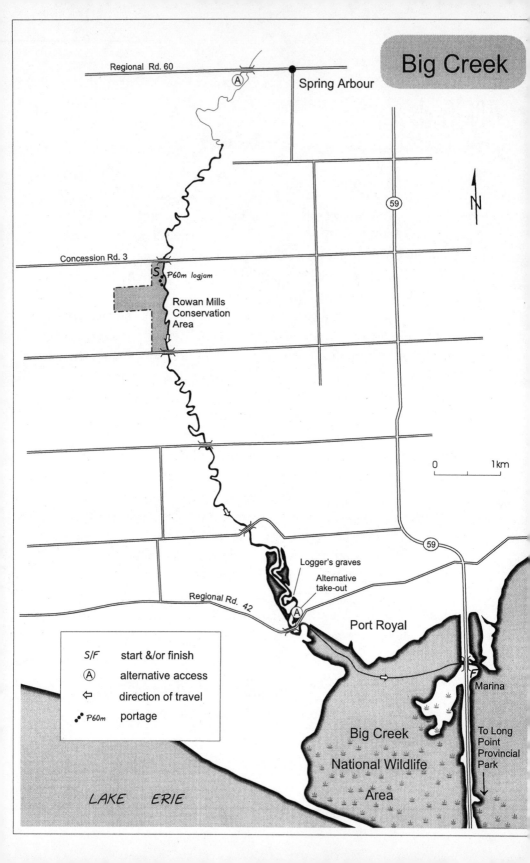

only portage is directly at the access, where a 60-meter trail along the right bank avoids a large clump of floating logs. From here the creek meanders its way through a jungle-like landscape, with giant willow, soft maple and centuries-old walnut trees crowding the muddy banks, all being slowly strangled by wild grape vines and long strands of Virginia creeper. Rare Carolinian species also grow along the shore — trees such as sassafras, chinquapin oak, tulip tree and pawpaw. Even with the great variety of bird species that can be sighted along the creek, I think it's the thick-forested banks that inspire me most on this route. Oddly enough, the creek was a regular highway for lumber back in the late 1800s. In fact, Port Royal was a major shipping center that saw millions of dollars' worth of pine and oak sent to markets around the world. The cemetery in Port Royal, located directly beside Big Creek, is the final resting place for a number of loggers who drowned while clearing logjams. By 1880, the local trees were almost all gone. If it were not for the Long Point Company, who owned most of the land in the area, refusing to allow any further cutting, the banks of Big Creek would have eroded away completely.

The only hard part of traveling this section of Big Creek is figuring out when to paddle it. Spring and fall are your best options for catching the birds in peak migration, and for being assured of adequate water levels (the local tobacco farms tend to suck the creek dry by midsummer). Both seasons have their disadvantages, though. Spring floods can make maneuvering around sweepers (newly fallen debris) extremely dangerous. And come fall, the opening of hunting season can easily become a problem, especially in the Big Creek National Wildlife Area, established in 1978 as a "controlled" hunting zone, between Regional Road 42 and Regional Road 59. Even if you're wearing bright-colored clothes, a trip at that time could be considered suicidal. The early part of May or late September is probably best. It's the time when the birds are on the move, bugs are at their lowest, and trigger-happy hunters have yet to head out into the marsh for duck season.

Big Creek

Difficulty:
Novice to intermediate, depending on water levels and the number of logjams blocking the waterway

Portages:
One (a few lift-overs may also be necessary)

Longest portage:
60 meters

Fee:
No fee is required.

Alternative access:
Regional Road 60, just two concession roads north of the main access point, can be used to extend the route an extra hour and a half.

Alternative route:
You can plan a two-to-three-day route from the town of Delhi (campsites have yet to be established and logjams make the route difficult at times).

Kayak friendly:
A canoe is better suited for dealing with possible lift-overs.

Outfitters:
None

For more information:
LONG POINT CONSERVATION AUTHORITY
R.R. 3
Simcoe, Ontario
N3Y 4K2
519-428-4623

LONG POINT PROVINCIAL PARK
Box 99
Port Rowan, Ontario
N0E 1M0
519-586-2133
1-888-668-7275 (reservations)

Maps:
The Long Point Conservation Authority has produced a pamphlet, *Big Creek Canoe Route.*

Topographical maps:
Port Burwell 40 I/10, Long Point 40 I/9, Tillsonburg 40 I/15 and Simcoe 40 I/16

Thames River

Canoeing has always meant wilderness to me. So when my brother-in-law, Jim Harkin, and his two sons, Ryan and Keelan, asked me to take them canoeing on the Thames River — a not-so-wild waterway near their home in London and a good three-hour drive south of where I live in Peterborough — I couldn't help but feel a little hesitant, at first. During my years of canoeing rivers further north, I've grown used to remote places. The idea of paddling that close to development, past culverts spitting out tainted water and under major thoroughfares crowded with minivans holds little appeal: it's difficult for me to swallow the philosophy that any place with water could mean interesting canoeing. In fact, my only reason for agreeing to take on this non-wilderness route (the most southern watercourse in Canada) was that I had promised to take my nephews canoeing for a number of years, and they finally called me on it. So, keeping an open mind, I headed south with my wife, Alana, to guide Jim, Ryan and Keelan on their very first canoe trip, which, surprisingly, became one of my best times spent in a canoe all season.

The Thames River, originating northeast of London and flowing southwesterly to Lake St. Clair, offers more than 300 kilometers of navigable waterway. The upper river, between St. Mary's Dam and the city of London, is a quick stretch of water that remains confined by steep valley slopes. This is considered the most scenic portion of the river. By mid-June, however, the north branch quickly becomes a dried-up boulder garden. The lower half, named "La Tranche" by early French-Canadian explorers because of its wide, ditch-like appearance, begins south of the town of Delaware and is mostly characterized by a slow current bordered by cornfields and dusty country roads. It's an easy all-season paddle but most canoeists find it quite

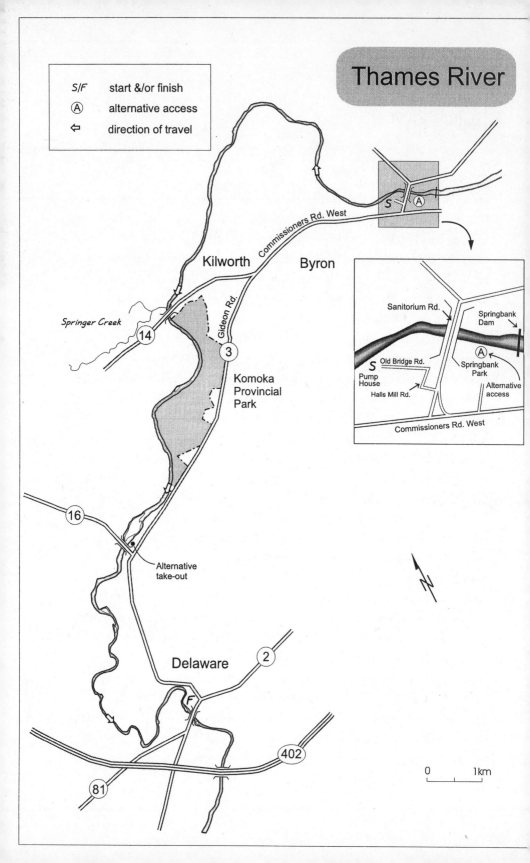

Thames River

S/F   start &/or finish

Ⓐ   alternative access

⇐   direction of travel

Commissioners Rd. West

Kilworth

Byron

Springer Creek

14

Gideon Rd.

3

Komoka Provincial Park

16

Alternative take-out

Delaware

2

F

402

81

0   1km

N

S

Ⓐ

Inset

Sanitorium Rd.

Springbank Dam

Old Bridge Rd.

S

Pump House

Halls Mill Rd.

Springbank Park

Alternative access

Commissioners Rd. West

Brother-in-law Jim Harkin and nephews Keelan and Ryan (Thames River).

dull at times. Our group chose what's in-between — a 19-kilometer section of shallow swifts and deep forested banks, beginning just below London's Springbank Dam and ending before the town of Delaware, along Highway 2. It was a perfect choice for us, first because it was more navigable than the north branch and much more natural than the lower half; and second, the access point happened to be only three blocks away from my brother-in-law's house.

To reach the put-in, head south on Sanitorium Road and make a right on Halls Mill Road, and then a left on Old Bridge Road. There is a parking area beside a pump house, and a rough road heads down to the launch area. To shuttle a second vehicle to the take-out on the east side of Highway 2, drive back to Sanitorium Road and turn right onto Commissioners Road West. Approximately 3 kilometers south, make a left onto Gideon Road (County Road 3), and then eventually a right on to Highway 2. The parking area is on the northeast side of the bridge.

Saving us the hassles of a shuttle (the plague of any river route), we were fortunate to have my sister, Sharon, who agreed not only to drop us off at the put-in but also to pick us up at the end of the day. She even made a promise to drive us to the nearest fast-food restaurant for an order of burgers and fries if we came back in one piece.

The gang stops once again to stretch their legs (Komoka Provincial Park, Thames River).

Only a few meters downstream is the first of many boulder swifts found between here and Delaware. To me and Alana, the fast water didn't seem quick enough to worry about and we decided that the calm stretch just before the drop would be a good place to show our novice canoe-mates a few paddling techniques before heading down the river. All three of them listened attentively to our description of pries, cross draws and back ferries. All was well, until their canoe began drifting backward toward the rapid. Alana and I began screaming out the proper strokes needed to swing the canoe back around. Completely dumbfounded at their predicament, they gawked at us as if we were speaking some type of foreign language and proceeded to head backward down current. Then, as their canoe came uncomfortably close to the foot of the drop, my sister, who was still watching us from the landing, yelled out a reminder of her fast-food pledge. Well, I've never seen two young paddlers try so hard to keep a canoe upright. The boat still shot through all the foam and froth in complete reverse but they all remained dry. Sharon then threw in a chocolate milkshake with her promise of burgers and fries and we waved her a goodbye and continued downriver.

There was a set of fast water about every kilometer or so throughout the day, and each time we would make a point of deciding which channel held less rock and more water. When in doubt, the rule was to choose the outside bend and make sure to keep the canoe pointed downstream.

We were thankful there were no other serious mishaps, nothing, that is, unless you count nearly being hit by a golf ball coming from the London Hunt and Country Club, becoming entangled in a not-so-polite angler's fishing line while he was busy landing one of the biggest catches of his life, or being attacked by a gathering of half-crazed Canada geese.

Apart from the odd development encroaching on the river and the half-tame waterfowl, I was totally impressed with the wildness of the river. By the time we reached the County Road 14 bridge, our group had spotted five great blue herons, two belted kingfishers, an

Keelan works on his clamshell collection.

osprey, a longnose gar (a fish similar to a pike but with an elongated nose), and half a dozen turtles — including one of the rare Eastern softshell turtle. Surprisingly, the Thames River is home to forty percent of Canada's endangered species and, in fact, holds more species of plants and animals today than when the aboriginals first settled here in A.D. 500.

We eventually stopped for lunch on a gravel bar just upstream from Kilworth and the County Road 14 bridge. As Alana and I prepared the sandwiches and boiled a pot of tea, the two boys dragged their father down the shoreline to search for more wildlife — actually, I think they both had to pee and were too embarrassed to mention the matter in front of Alana. A few minutes later the group of inquisitive naturalists returned with a collection of clamshells. The banks were littered with them, so I wasn't too surprised with their discovery. What I found amazing, however, was the diversity in species the boys had gathered from one area — wart-back, false pig-toe and pocketbook, to list just a few.

Actually, between 1920 and 1940, the Thames River was considered the richest clamshell bed in all of Canada and was heavily harvested for the commercial production of pearl buttons. In fact, it was recorded that the shell beds were so thick in the Thames that the yield was six to ten clams per square foot. The workers, able only to collect them by hand, received 25 cents per bushel when the water was warm and 75 cents when the water was cold. If they were lucky, the pickers would find a pearl formation and sell it for $5 an ounce. Eventually casein, a by-product of milk, was more commonly used in the making of buttons, and so the clamshell industry ended on the Thames River by 1946.

Downstream from our lunch spot, where the shoreline slowly changes over from gravel shoals to steep clay banks housing hundreds of bank swallows, Komoka Provincial Park (located on the left) offered a second place for the gang to stretch their legs, gather more clamshells, and sneak away from Alana again.

It was a long break. My nephews seemed to prefer taking extended walks along the shoreline to sitting in a cramped canoe and paddling. So by late afternoon we had only managed to reach the County Road 16 bridge, a good hour away from the main take-out along Highway 2. When I informed them that this wasn't the proper take-out spot, Ryan and Keelan began to whine a little about another hour of paddling before satisfying their fast-food craving. That's when Jim, obviously an experienced parent, took over the trip itinerary. Pulling out his cell phone from his daypack, he called my sister for an early pickup at the County Road 16 bridge rather than Highway 2. A half-hour later the intrepid canoeists, Ryan and Keelan, were standing in line at McDonalds ordering a large fries to go with their burgers, informing the server that they were extra hungry from paddling in the wilderness all day. I didn't dare laugh at them. After all, in their minds, the Thames was a wild river and I wasn't about to spoil their party. Instead, I made a solid promise that Alana and I would return next year to take them on the even more remote branch north of the city — as long as we all wore helmets to defend ourselves against flying golf balls, that is.

Thames River

Difficulty:
Novice route with some swift water that can be easily negotiated

Portages: None

Fee: No fee is required.

Alternative access:
Canoeists can put in directly below Springbank Dam instead of at the pump house and take out earlier at either County Road 14 or County Road 16.

Alternative route:
A number of other daytrips can be had on the north branch and the Lower Thames River. Contact the Upper Thames River Conservation Authority for information.

Kayak friendly: Yes

Outfitters:
NOVACKS
211 King Street
London, Ontario
N6A 1C9
519-434-2282

For more information:
LONDON CANOE CLUB
Box 21016
Southcrest Post Office
390 Springbank Drive
London, Ontario
N6J 4W2
519-473-2582
The club rents canoes out of their boathouse just upstream of Springbank Dam.

THE UPPER THAMES RIVER
CONSERVATION AUTHORITY
R.R. 6
London, Ontario
N6A 4C1
519-451-2800

Maps:
The Upper Thames River Conservation Authority has produced a pamphlet, *The Upper Thames Canoe Route: St. Marys to Delaware.*

Topographical maps:
London 40 I/14

Grand River

In 1994 the Grand River was designated a Canadian Heritage River. It was a special event, especially because the Grand was the first urban river given this extra status, and designated primarily for its human history and not its natural surroundings.

It's true this Southern Ontario river holds a strong connection with our past, something easily witnessed by paddling past the Scottish stonemasonry of Fergus or under the wooden covered bridge at West Montrose. Yet the Grand also holds plenty of natural heritage to explore. In fact, one-fifth of the river remains in an almost wild state. The section traveled most frequently by canoeists is from Cambridge to Paris — a 20-kilometer stretch of river that winds its way past scenic cliffs, wide floodplains and an almost undeveloped strip of Carolinian forest.

Apart from its wild splendor, the Cambridge to Paris route also has quite a few added advantages for canoeists. The short length of river means it takes only three to four hours to complete. Low water levels discourage motorboat traffic but the river is still navigable for canoes all season long. The route is also extremely easy to access, with a choice of three outfitters near the take-out in Paris that provide a convenient shuttle service as well as boat rentals.

It was in Cambridge itself that the Grand received its official designation as a Canadian Heritage River. It was the largest ceremony in the history of the Canadian Heritage Rivers System and gave tribute to a new strategy of river stewardship that has helped set a precedent for how we will manage our waterways in the future.

The preferred put-in is just south of Cambridge on Highway 24. The launch site is on the right side, between the GTO Gas Bar and the trailhead for the Cambridge to Paris Rail Trail. (The trail uses the abandoned railbed for the electric "interurban" railway line built

Kathy and John — and my canoe — survive another dunking in the Grand River.

in 1915.) Whether you are organizing your own shuttle or paying one of the outfitters, you must first drive to the take-out point, however. Continue south on Highway 24 to East River Road. When you reach Paris, use one of the parking areas just inside the town limits, between Willow and Elm Streets or at Elm and Grand River Road West.

Immediately beyond the put-in, the Carolinian forest grows thick along the banks. Sassafras, sycamore and shagbark hickory —

all trees growing at the northern limits of their range — dominate the landscape. The remains of even rarer habitats — old prairie grassland, savannah oak and miniature bogs formed in kettle depressions — co-exist alongside them. This wide range of shoreline habitats, from marsh to upland forests, holds an abundance of wildlife, including the southern flying squirrel and opossums, Ontario's only marsupial. But it's the river itself that boasts the highest number of species. Eighty-five different kinds of fish, ranging from rainbow trout migrating upstream from Lake Erie to the less glamorous "mudcat" (catfish) that lives all year round in the silty estuaries, can be found swimming in the Grand River, making it home to more species than any other river in Ontario.

Signs of the Grand River's rich human culture are also visible along various sections. Archeological evidence is constantly being uncovered along the riverbanks, giving evidence that native cultures were here as long as 11,000 years ago to hunt mastodon and bison. You can admire old cobblestone architecture in the ruins of a mill site near the town of Glen Morris and the massive stone abutments used to support the CNR bridge crossing the river just upriver from Paris.

The Grand River is rated as a novice canoe route, but there's still quite a bit of whitewater to contend with, ranging from rock-strewn swifts during low water conditions to manageable Class I rapids in moderate to high water levels. The most noteworthy set is just downstream of Glen Morris at a place called Spottiswood Bluffs. The rapids come up quickly when you turn left around the high bank, and canoeists have to be ready to guide themselves through the rough parts.

Personally, I find the shallow rock gardens just before the take-out in Paris far more difficult to maneuver through than the set at Spottiswood Bluffs, especially in low water conditions. In fact, during my last outing on the Grand, while guiding the gang from Boston Mills Press, I ended the trip with one severely damaged boat.

It was John and Kathy who accidentally hit the rock broadside. With the canoe leaning upstream, they allowed gallons of water to

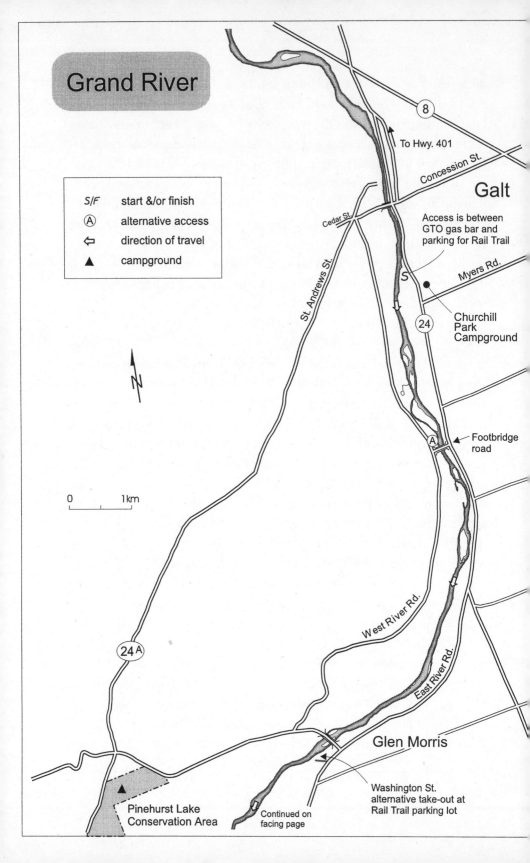

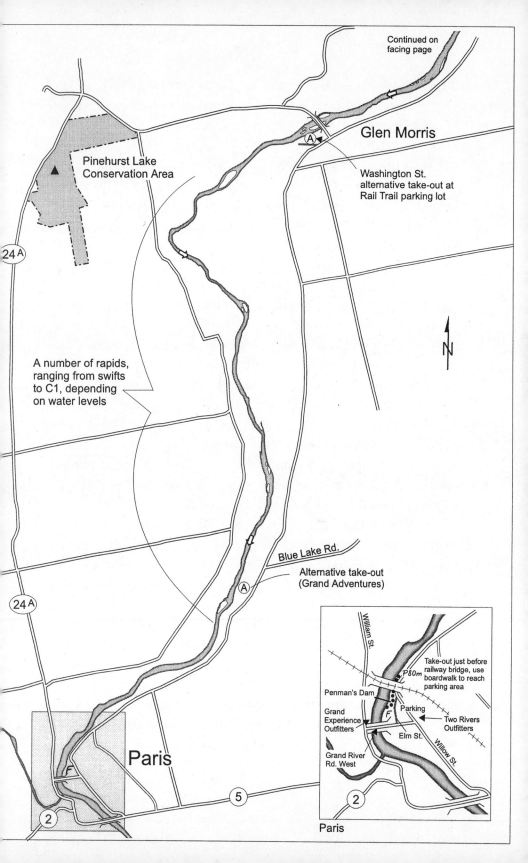

Continued on facing page

Pinehurst Lake
Conservation Area

24 A

A number of rapids,
ranging from swifts
to C1, depending
on water levels

Glen Morris

Washington St.
alternative take-out at
Rail Trail parking lot

N

24 A

Blue Lake Rd.

Alternative take-out
(Grand Adventures)

Paris

5

2

William St.

Take-out just before
railway bridge, use
boardwalk to reach
parking area

P 80m

Penman's Dam

Parking

Grand
Experience
Outfitters

Two Rivers
Outfitters

Elm St.

Grand River
Rd. West

Willow St.

2

Paris

flush into the canoe. In seconds the plastic boat wrapped itself completely around the boulder and the occupants were forced to stand in waist-deep water until my partner, Noel, and I could paddle out to rescue them.

The entire scene was actually quite comical. Noel and I almost wedged our canoe on the same rock while attempting to eddy in behind it. Then, while all four of us tried to free the canoe, barking out commands at one another, it suddenly freed itself and began floating down to the next pile of rocks. We eventually lassoed the canoe with a throw-rope before it became stuck again and even managed to bend the thing back in shape, enough anyway for Kathy and John to paddle it at least to the take-out in Paris.

In retrospect, the incident, though it was a sobering one, had a positive side to it. Even though I had one of my favourite canoes permanently scarred, and may never be able to use it again, my partner and I now had something to tease John and Kathy about. You see, ever since Noel and I dumped in a rapid on the Mattawa River a couple of years ago, we have been regularly reminded of our mishap by John and Kathy. Now it's our turn. And the best part of it is that Noel and I upset in a technical Class II rapid on a wild northern river, not in a mere swift on a suburban waterway. And yes, our canoe came out of it without a single scratch.

Apart from the slight chance of damaging your boat on the rapids en route, the only true danger on the Grand comes while approaching the finishing point in Paris. A deadly sluice has formed below Penman's Dam and is located not far downstream from the take-out. This boiling water creates an extremely hazardous undertow and has been called the "drowning machine" by local canoeists. As long as you avoid traveling on the river during flood conditions, however, the approach to the take-out is quite safe. When coming into town, just make sure to stay close to the left shoreline and watch for the landing marked immediately before the railway bridge. A wooden staircase and boardwalk will safely lead you to the familiar take-out point at the corner of Willow and Elm Streets.

Grand River

Time: 1 day (3 to 4 hours)

Difficulty:
Novice to intermediate due to numerous swifts encountered between Glen Morris and Paris that could be challenging in high water levels.

Portages: None

Fee: No fee is required.

Alternative access:
An alternative put-in is where Footbridge Road crosses the river, not far downstream from the GTO Gas Bar. A second parking area for the Rail Trail in Glen Morris is located to the west of East River Road, at the end of Washington Street, and it can also be used as an alternative put-in or take-out.

Alternative route:
Most of the swifts can be avoided by taking out in Glen Morris.

Kayak friendly: Yes

Outfitters:
ADVENTURES ON THE GRAND
Box 555
147 East River Road
Paris, Ontario N3L 3T6

519-442-1449
519-442-1447
1-800-355-5358

TWO RIVERS VARIETY
79 Willow Street
Paris, Ontario N3L 2K9
519-442-2415
800-350-2268

GRAND EXPERIENCES
113 Grand River Street
Paris, Ontario N3L 2M4
519-442-3654
888-258-0441

For more information:
GRAND RIVER CONSERVATION AUTHORITY
Box 729, 400 Clyde Road
Cambridge, Ontario N1R 5W6
519-621-2761

Maps:
The Grand River Conservation Authority has produced a guidebook, *Canoeing on the Grand River*, which covers the entire river from Belwood Lake to Lake Erie.

Topographical maps:
Brantford 40 P/1
Kitchener 40 P/8

Rockwood Lake Conservation Area

After three years of mishaps, the Boston Mills gang, my publishing company for the past ten years, made the group decision that last year's annual canoe trip would be reduced to an easy daytrip on Rockwood Lake, situated only ten minutes away from their office in Erin.

John, the publisher, was looking forward to just paddling an hour or so and then heading back to the village of Rockwood for a gourmet meal at La Vielle Auberge rather than repeating the year before's two ten-hour days that ended only with prepackaged freeze-dried dinners. Noel, the chief editor, was glad that the manmade millponds had no dangerous whitewater to dump in (back in 1997, he and I upset our canoe in a technical Class II rapid on the Mattawa River). And Kathy, the second editor in charge, was ecstatic that she didn't have to deal with the same bugs, bad weather, nuisance bear reports, and grueling portages of Algonquin's 1996 trip.

Don't get me wrong. The chance to miss out on misadventure wasn't the only reason we chose to go paddling for the day at Rockwood Conservation Area. It happens to be one of the most unique parks in Southern Ontario, and boasts a variety of geological wonders — towering limestone cliffs, caves, and an impressive collection of glacial potholes (including the world's largest pothole, known as the Devil's Well). Between the two large millponds, where only non-motorized boating is allowed, are the rustic remains of an old woolen mill that can be explored. There's definitely a strong appeal to this not so out-of-the-way treasure.

The town of Rockwood is located 12 kilometers northeast of Guelph, along Highway 7, and Rockwood Conservation Area is just

Facing page: Towering limestone cliffs are just one of the attractions that make Rockwood Lake a great weekend getaway.

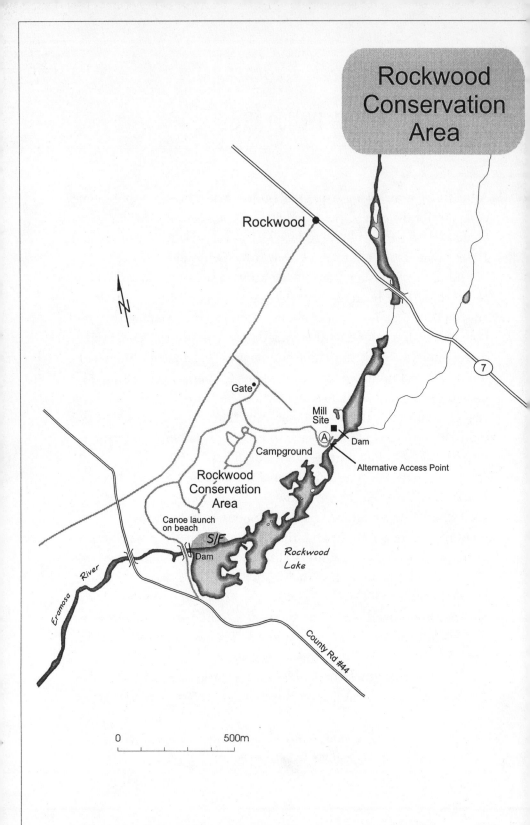

Rockwood
Conservation
Area

Rockwood

7

N

Gate

Mill
Site

A

Dam

Campground

Alternative Access Point

Rockwood
Conservation
Area

Canoe launch
on beach

S/F

Dam

Rockwood
Lake

Eramosa River

County Rd #44

0   500m

We came by canoe — definitely the best way to explore Rockwood Lake Conservation Area.

outside of town, south of Highway 7. Considering the park's small size (79 hectares), it has quite a lot to offer visitors, including 45 serviced and 55 unserviced campsites, three group camping areas, as well a swimming and picnic area. A good system of trails leads to the most significant potholes, the ruins of the old mill, and scenic lookouts on both sides of the Eramosa River, which bisects the conservation area. The best way to get around, however, is by canoe.

The put-in is at the beach area on the western end of the south pond. From here, either spend your time fishing for bass or rainbow trout across from the beach or paddle east to the shallower, quieter portion of the park, and to the site of the old mill.

To reach the top end of the pond, and the mill site, you must navigate through the labyrinth of irregular limestone, made up of collapsed and eroded potholes formed when boulders became trapped in the swirling eddies of flooded glacial meltwaters and then began to cut into the soft limestone. It would take approximately a thousand years to form a bowl-sized hole. To form the almost 200 potholes at Rockwood, which average 6 meters wide and 12 meters deep, it would have taken more than ten thousand years.

The geology of the area is quite unlike that of the surrounding farmland thanks to the Eramosa River. In the course of time, the river has cut through the deep soils deposited by the passing glaciers and exposed a portion of the neighboring Niagara Escarpment.

When the community of Rockwood was originally settled by Quakers, this same rock was used extensively to built their homes, churches and schools, some of which still stand today. The woolen mill between the two millponds, built with the ancient limestone, was established by Richard Harris in 1867 and expanded in 1884. The mill operated until 1919, reopened for a short while in the 1930s to provide uniforms for the Canadian army, and was then purchased by the conservation authority in 1959.

A fire in 1965 destroyed most of the building, and through the years, vandalism has plagued some of the park's other attractions. (Some idiot painted fake pictographs on a cliff face on the lower pond.) The conservation authority, however, is now busy with a restoration project to the 19th-century stone mill, and local businesses in town have donated money to help regenerate the natural areas of the park. By doing so, both groups have made a sound investments in two vital and important elements of our past, as well as a great daytrip for not-so-adventurous canoeists looking to escape work for the day.

Facing page: A woolen mill established in 1867 (Rockwood Lake Conservation Area).

Rockwood Lake Conservation Area

Time: 1 day (2 hours)

Difficulty: Novice

Portages: None

Fee:
A permit must be purchased at the main gatehouse.

Alternative access:
It is possible to drive directly down to the old mill site and launch your canoe from there.

Alternative route: No

Kayak friendly: Yes

Outfitters:
The main campground offers canoe rentals.

For more information:
GRAND RIVER CONSERVATION AUTHORITY
Box 729
400 Clyde Road
Cambridge, Ontario
N1R 5W6
519-621-2761
519-856-9543 (Rockwood Conservation Area)

Topographic Maps:
Guelph 40 P/9

 Credit River

From its source, high on top of the Niagara Escarpment, to its abrupt ending at Lake Ontario, the Credit River cuts through half a dozen towns, dips under three major expressways, and bypasses countless subdivisions, streetlights and fast-food restaurants. Surprisingly, however, this suburban waterway still holds enough wild places to make for an enjoyable paddle, my favorite being the relaxed, 16-kilometer daytrip between the towns of Terra Cotta and Norval.

Terra Cotta is located along County Road 19 (Winston Churchill Boulevard), approximately 20 kilometers north of Highway 401, and the best put-in is the parking lot of the Terra Cotta Inn (be sure to ask for permission to park first). To organize a car shuttle, drop off a second vehicle 10 kilometers south of Terra Cotta, at Norval's Canoe Country Outfitters (905-846-5000), also located along Winston Churchill Boulevard, on the southeast side of the river.

Other than the car shuttle, the most difficult part about organizing a trip down this section of the Credit is deciding when to paddle it. In the summer drought, you may end up walking more than paddling; during a spring flood, the many swifts encountered along the way (the first being directly out from the put-in) can be navigable only by extreme whitewater canoeists. Years ago a high-school friend asked me to be his partner in an annual spring race on the Upper Credit. After spending the day dodging sweepers, splashing through haystack waves, and even traveling down the river backward a couple of times after we struck a boulder and spun around, it must have been pure luck that we survived the whole ordeal, let alone went home with second prize.

Facing page, top: A view of the Credit River from Glen Williams Bridge.
Bottom: The town of Glen Williams welcomes visitors with a quaint
restaurant, art boutiques and an old-style brew pub.

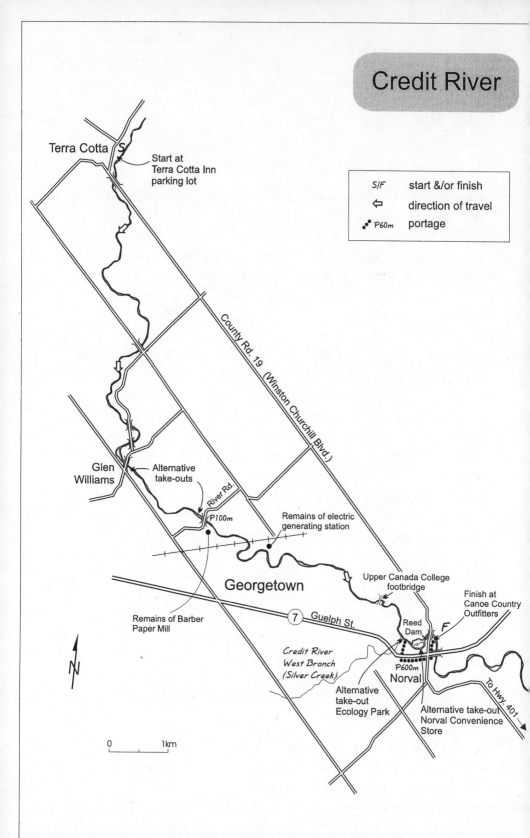

Credit River

Terra Cotta *S*

Start at
Terra Cotta Inn
parking lot

S/F start &/or finish
⇐ direction of travel
•••• *P60m* portage

County Rd. 19 (Winston Churchill Blvd.)

Glen
Williams → Alternative
take-outs

River Rd.

P100m

Remains of electric
generating station

Georgetown

Upper Canada College
footbridge

Finish at
Canoe Country
Outfitters

Remains of Barber
Paper Mill

7 Guelph St.

Reed
Dam *F*

*Credit River
West Branch
(Silver Creek)*

P600m

Norval

N

Alternative
take-out
Ecology Park

Alternative take-out
Norval Convenience
Store

To Hwy 401

0   1km

Ideally, the best time to paddle the route is sometime between mid-May and late June. Even a late-season run is possible after a few days of hard rain. Just be sure to keep the boat pointed in the right direction (downriver) if the current picks up.

Most rapids en route occur between the hamlets of Terra Cotta and Glen Williams. Here, the river lies along an old glacial spillway and either flushes over large beds of sand and gravel left by the glacier or cuts deep into banks to expose the layers of red shale that once lined the shores of an ancient sea. This soft bedrock, known as the Queenstone shale, gave Terra Cotta (a Latin term for "baked earth") its present name. Originally, the name of the town was Salmonville for the great number of Atlantic salmon that would head up from Lake Ontario to spawn. But with the building of gristmills all along the Credit River, the traditional migration route was blocked, and by 1890 the salmon were altogether extinct. Around the same time, the Plewes family took advantage of the local red clay deposits to operate a brick kiln. Soon the brickworks prospered, and in 1902 the name was officially changed.

Before reaching Glen Williams (a small village equipped with a quaint restaurant, art boutiques and an old-style brew pub), the river passes under three roadside bridges, a few cow barns, and some suburban backyards tamed with manicured lawns and well-kept gardens. Overall, the deep valley is heavily forested, and this first quarter of the route is the best place to watch for wildlife.

Approximately one kilometer past Glen Williams, the river passes through Georgetown, where River Road provides a possible take-out spot if you wish to reduce the trip to under three hours. In doing so, however, you miss one of the best historic sites on the river. Just downstream, where a 100-meter portage is marked to the left of an old concrete dam (it is possible to carefully run the rapids here), are the remains of the Barber Paper Mill. The Barber Brothers, whose descendants also build the first Canadian electric generating station in 1888, 2 kilometers downstream (just beyond the massive iron railway bridge) constructed the mill in 1837.

The remaining stretch of river downstream of the historic mill and the generating station site is also worth the extra hour or two of paddling. Most of the land adjacent to the Credit is owned by Upper Canada College and is kept relatively wild. A good current, formed between the high red-clay banks and around several large islands, also makes for some interesting paddling up until where a metal footbridge spans the river.

Once past the footbridge, however, the current grows sluggish, and it seems to take forever to reach the outskirts of Norval. Eventually, two prominent No Trespassing signs appear, posted on both sides of the river, and you're faced with the major disadvantage of any suburban waterway — landowner disputes.

This particular conflict at Norval has been going on for years now, with the critical point of debate, between the canoeists' right to portage and the landowners' right to privacy, occurring in 1989. Canoe Ontario and Jim Greenacre of the Wilderness Canoe Association took the property owners (Julian and Laurie Reed) to court for blocking the river with barbed-wire fence and refusing the right to portage around a concrete dam built in the middle of the private property. The plaintiff's main argument was that the Credit River remained a navigable waterway. The defendant (Mr. Reed) firmly stated, however, that the recreationists who use the river do not pay proper heed to the needs of those who live and work on the adjoining property (garbage has been left on the landowner's property and, on occasion, he and his family have been verbally abused by people traveling the river).

Both parties obviously have valid points. The history of the Credit River clearly shows that up to the latter part of the 18th century and the early part of the 19th century, it was used as a regular highway for personal and commercial transportation. Then, after a brief spell as a log-floating route, the river quickly became a favorite destination for recreational canoeists. These points prove that the Credit River was, and still is, navigable. However, the land was originally sold by the Crown in 1822 to the landowner's maternal

At least this family of Canada geese doesn't have to worry about dealing with landowner disputes while traveling along the Credit River.

great-grandfather. The dam, the first constructed along the Credit, was put in place in 1825. For over 35 years, the landowner has made use of the dam (supposedly to generate electricity) and needed to place barbed-wire fence south of the dam to stop his cattle from wandering up and down the river when crossing to the opposite side to graze.

In the end, the Ontario Supreme Court judged that, since the Credit River is clearly a navigable and public waterway and the Crown patent did not grant title to the riverbed, the canoeists had a right to travel the section of river through the private property. The landowner therefore had to remove the barbed-wire fence. When dealing with the right to portage around the dam, the judge stated that the right of navigation does not necessarily imply a right to portage over private property and the landowner should not be made to sacrifice part of his property rights so the canoeists could more fully enjoy their public right of navigation. The right to portage was therefore declined.

In a nutshell, this means that you are limited to only a few options to get back to your vehicle parked at the outfitters once you reach the outskirts of Norval, and none of them happen to be as simple as portaging around Mr. Reed's dam.

The last time I paddled the river (June 1999), I noted two possible take-out points on the right bank, before the small millpond that has formed upstream of the dam. (Take note that one of the problems with river routes cursed by landowner disputes is that put-in and take-out points are constantly changing, so be sure to ask at the outfitters if any changes have occurred.) The first is at the Willow Park Ecology Center (a trailer park up until 1993), situated at the mouth of the West Branch of the Credit (sometimes called Silver Creek). The second is behind Norval Convenience Store (905-873-7104), located just downstream of the ecology park and past the Presbyterian church, built in 1888 and once home of the famous Canadian author of *Anne of Green Gables*, Lucy Maud Montgomery, from 1926 to 1935.

The park has a proper canoe launch just upstream on the West Branch. Craving a cold soda and a bag of salty potato chips, however, I chose the back of the convenience store to unload. I then took the five-minute walk east on Highway 7 (Guelph Street) and then north on Winston Churchill Boulevard (known as Adamson Street through the village), picked up my vehicle at Canoe Country Outfitters, and drove back to the store to pack up — all the time being gawked at by a frustrated Mr. Reed standing guard on his front porch.

At first I didn't mind Mr. Reed leering at me while I walked 600 meters through town rather than a mere 20 meters around his silly dam. I find it easier to use a bit of etiquette rather than act like some kind of rebel when dealing with oddballs like Reed. But then I heard him giggle at me — I least I think he was giggling at me — and suddenly I became a radical, yelling out, "Free the shackled river!"

I don't think this helped ease any of the animosity formed between Mr. Reed and the recreational canoeists. But boy, did it feel good! After all, why shouldn't the river be reborn again? The world of mill dams is long gone, and with the sluggish impoundment behind the concrete wall drained, the river would be able to flex and stretch for the first time in years, and maybe even bring back some wildness to this not-so-wild place.

Credit River

Time: 1 day

Difficulty:
Intermediate (numerous swifts are encountered)

Portages: 2

Longest portage:
600 meters (can be avoided by taking out just upstream at Ecology Park)

Fee: No fee is required.

Alternative access:
River Road in Georgetown and the county road bridge in Glen Williams make possible access points as well.

Alternative route:
The route can be shortened by taking out at Glen Williams or Georgetown and extended downstream to Huttonville.

Kayak friendly:
Only in high water levels

Outfitters:
CANOE COUNTRY OUTFITTERS
16 Adamson Street North
Box 209
Norval, Ontario
L0P 1K0
905-846-5000

For more information:
CREDIT VALLEY
CONSERVATION AUTHORITY
1255 Derry Road West
Meadowvale, Ontario
L5N 6R4
905-670-1615

Topographical maps:
Brampton 30 M/12

Nonquon River

The first time I experienced the Nonquon was during the Nonqoun River Canoe Race, an annual event held the first Saturday in June and sponsored by the Scugog Historical Society. I was partnered up with workmate Mark Williamson, and we found the race a lot of fun but didn't think too much of the river at the time. It seemed like an endless meander, an almost stagnant bit of water that was constantly interrupted by countless beaver dams and dead-end channels. In fact, the only reason we could imagine why over 200 people would gather in such a place for almost 30 years (the event is billed as the largest and longest-running canoe race in the province) was that the race itself became an annual excuse for canoeists to put their boats in the river.

Feeling guilty about our ill feelings toward the Nonquon, Mark and I became determined to give the river another try. This trip, it was important to have no set schedule and to travel at a much more leisurely pace. We also decided on a time when there was little chance of running into another person, especially not a gang of competitive and somewhat overenthusiastic racers. We chose the second weekend in December, which is usually a little late for canoe travel, but it was a mild winter and the lakes and rivers had yet to freeze over.

To organize the shuttle, we left Mark's vehicle near the mouth of the river at a parking area and boat launch just past the Mariposa Estate Park. (At the town of Seagrave, turn right off Highway 2 onto River Street, then right onto Sun Valley Road, and right again at Nonquon Drive.) During the canoe race the participants used

Facing page: One of the 200 paddlers who register for the annual Nonquon River Canoe Race.

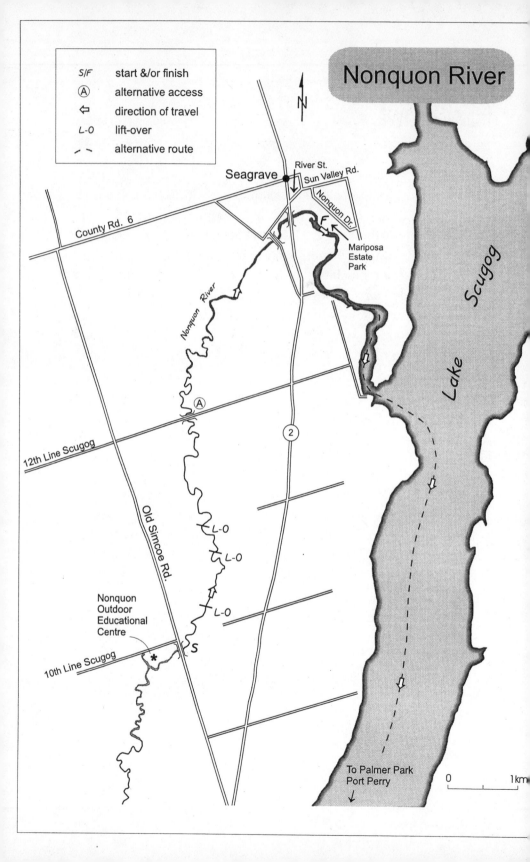

Palmer Park at Port Perry's waterfront as a take-out, making the race 26 kilometers in length, but Mark and I thought it would be unwise to paddle the lake section so late in the year so we chose the river mouth as an alternative finish. We then headed west on County Road 6 (just north of Seagrave), turned south on Old Simcoe Road, and 6 kilometers along, past Scugog Township Line 10 and the turn-off for the Nonquon Environmental Education Centre, we put in beside the river bridge.

Mark and I took half a day to paddle the same section of river that lasted just under two hours during the canoe race. There were some advantages to our much slower pace, of course. Not only did I take time out to plan for the next year's race, locating the best and quickest route through the network of passageways that spread through the middle section of river (when in doubt, keep to the right), but Mark and I also had plenty of time to explore the incredibly diverse marshland that surrounded the river as well. Now and then we could catch a glimpse of a cornfield or the top of a farmer's barn, but for the most part the swamp, managed as a provincial wildlife reserve by the Ministry of Natural Resources, kept us distant from any outside development. At the same time, the concealed area also provided a haven for wildlife. On one section of the bank, Mark and I counted three separate sets of animal tracks — the staggered pad marks of a coyote, the cloven hoof of a white-tailed deer, and the distinct tail drag of a muskrat.

Except for the half-dozen lift-overs to deal with, the trip itself was a breeze. There was no real current to contend with along the entire stretch of the Nonquon. The speed just picked up anytime the river passed over a poorly constructed beaver dam or a buildup of logs. The only real major issue to contend with was the lack of a solid shoreline to step out on and stretch our legs. Much of the river is entrenched in swamp, and it wasn't until after we'd passed under a bridge about three quarters of the way along that the banks were solid enough to hold our weight without caving in on themselves. We had to resort to having our tea and sandwiches while sitting in the canoe. And when

A provincial wildlife reserve has kept most of the Nonqoun River well protected from outside development.

we had to pee, one of us would steady the canoe while the other stood up and leaned over the side. We'd done exactly the same thing during the canoe race, though for a lesser cause. This time I kept my legs cramped and my bladder full as long as possible to enjoy the view, not to see how fast I could pass it by.

Nonquon River

Time: 1 day (3 to 5 hours)

Difficulty: Novice

Portages: None

Fee:
No fee is required. (There is a registration fee for the annual canoe race.)

Alternative access:
Scugog Line 12

Alternative route:
The trip can be shortened to less than two hours by taking out at the Scugog Line 12 bridge or extended by paddling south on Scugog Lake to Palmer Park in Port Perry.

Kayak friendly:
Yes (in fact, the canoe race has a separate registration for kayaks)

Outfitters: None

For more information:
SCUGOG INFORMATION CENTRE
269 Queen Street
Port Perry, Ontario
L9L 1B1
905-985-4971

SCUGOG SHORES HISTORICAL MUSEUM
905-985-3589

Topographical maps:
Scugog 31 D/2

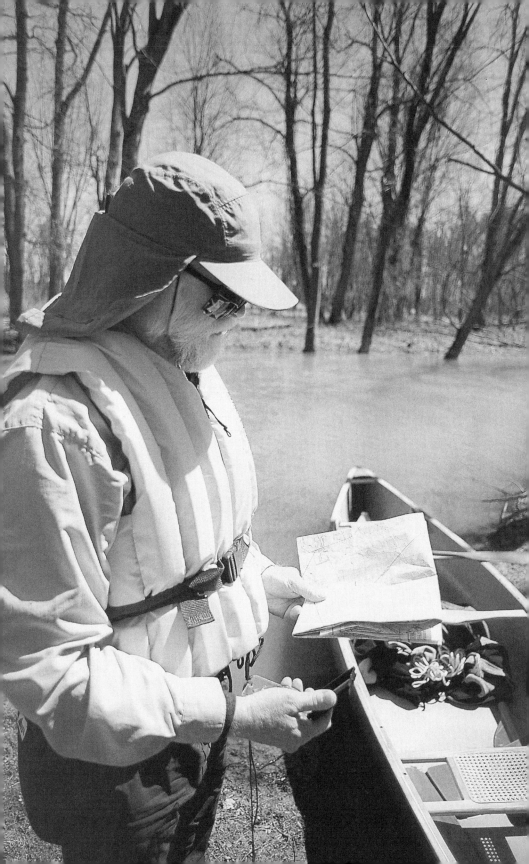

Minesing Swamp

Over the years I've heard a number of canoeists raving about spring paddling on Minesing Swamp — a 6,000-hectare wetland just west of Barrie. Personally, I had a difficult time seeing the thrill in paddling through a giant patch of stagnant water, especially during prime bug season, and it wasn't until last year that I decided to head out and see what all the fuss was about. I partnered up with Brian MacFadzan, a co-worker from Sir Sandford Fleming College, and to avoid the bug problem, we chose one of those warm spring days in early April when the mosquitoes have yet to hatch and high water levels make the swamp totally accessible.

The usual plan for exploring Minesing Swamp is to follow the Nottawasaga River, which flows almost directly through the middle of the wetland. The best put-in is located just north of Angus, on the east side of the Highway 90 bridge. The designated take-out is at Edanvale Conservation Authority, on the west side of the Highway 26 bridge. But this route takes a full day to paddle, and since Brian and I didn't arrive until well after 10 A.M., we chose to begin at Edanvale Conservation Authority and simply paddle upstream on the Nottawasaga River as far as Willow Creek and return via the same route. In doing so, we were able to avoid the hassles of a car shuttle (we had only one vehicle with us, anyway) as well as the only two portages en route, located just above the confluence of the Nottawasaga River and Willow Creek.

There was a strong current before and after the highway bridge, and at first, Brian and I wondered if upstream travel was actually

Facing page: Brian checks out the map and compass once again to help find our way through the flooded-out forest of Minesing Swamp.

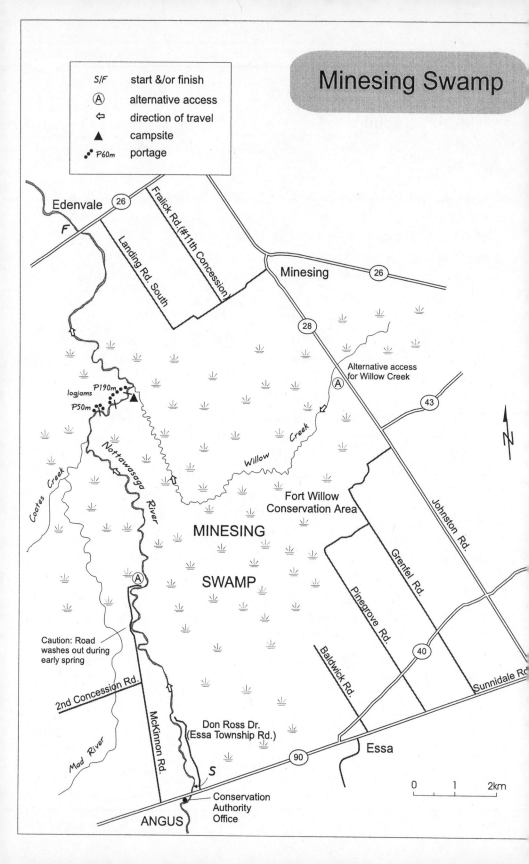

possible on the river. Eventually, however, the waterway expanded, flooding over the neighboring farm fields and through a massive stand of silver maple. The flow soon slowed to a crawl and the area seemed more like the Florida Everglades or Georgia's Okefenokee Swamp than some rural wetland in Southern Ontario. At times, Brian and I even found ourselves lost in the flooded-out forest and had to resort to our map and compass skills to find our way back to the Nottawasaga.

It took two and a half hours of paddling to reach where Willow Creek flows into the Nottawasaga River. Here, Brian and I took full advantage of finally having a dry place to get out and stretch our legs. We walked the two portages on the west side of the Nottawasaga, the first measuring 190 meters and the second only 50 meters. Both trails avoid extensive logjams that have clogged the river for so long that trees have taken root on top of the sun-bleached snags.

We then returned to the juncture of the two waterways and had lunch on the only well-used campsite en route. It's obvious that few people choose to camp overnight in a place so overwhelmed by floods. However, I do know a fellow canoeist, Rolf Kraiker, who has invented a unique way to spend the night out in Minesing. Rather than search for a cut of dry land, Rolf simply lashes a slab of plywood on top of two canoes and places his tent in the middle of the wooden platform. It's an ingenious way to spend the night in an area so overrun by water — so long as you're not prone to sleepwalking!

After lunch, Brian and I figured we had some time to explore Willow Creek before heading back down the river. This was the same waterway used by Lt. Col. Robert McDougall and the Glengarry Light Infantry to float a flotilla of boats, built at Fort Willow located further upstream on the Black Creek, to relieve the British garrison at Fort Michilimackinac in May 1814. Some canoeists have spent hours along this side creek each spring in search of any remains of Fort Willow. A group of local historians makes an annual pilgrimage down Willow Creek from Grenfel Road to celebrate McDougall's journey. Brian and I chose to spend our time enjoying the area's natural history instead. As we pushed our way upstream, with the creek itself disappearing and the entire area becoming one giant saturated forest, the swamp quickly became alive with various species of wildlife. Above us flew marsh hawks, ospreys, turkey vultures, a wide assortment of waterfowl, and a large number of great blue herons (Minesing Swamp holds Southern Ontario's largest heron rockery). We even heard a gathering of sand-hill cranes dancing away in a nearby fen and caught a glimpse of all three types of woodpeckers (downy, hairy and pileated). Down below, in the water, we spotted snapping turtles, huge carp and a few walleye, who, oddly enough, choose to spawn in the marsh rather than the gravel beds out on the river. Brian snapped a photo of a lone porcupine marooned up in the crook of a hackberry tree, patiently waiting for the water to recede.

This entire area, as well as the banks of the Nottawasaga River, quickly becomes impassable by mid-May, taken over by thick vegetation, low water levels, and zillions of mosquitoes. This happens to be the saving grace for the area's wildlife, however. For most of the breeding season, the 206 species of birds, 23 species of mammals, and more than 400 species of plants, ranging from Carolinian species to vegetation more commonly found in the Hudson Bay Lowlands, exist in a remote setting that is considered internationally important, and is now protected under the Ramsar Convention Act.

Brian and I actually enjoyed paddling Willow Creek more than the Nottawasaga River. Every time we made the decision to turn back toward the mouth of the creek, we would spot some rare bird or catch a glimpse of another gigantic snapping turtle and we would continue on to investigate. Eventually though, after becoming incredibly lost and having to depend on a series of snowmobile trail signs nailed to the trees to lead us back to the Nottawasaga River, we had to make the decision to call it quits and head back downstream to Edenvale. Surprisingly, the return trip only took us half the time.

This wasn't bad considering we found ourselves lost again after deciding to take another shortcut through the trees and then became windbound for a good half-hour while paddling across the last cornfield of the day.

Minesing Swamp

Time: 1 day (4 to 5 hours)

Difficulty:
Novice to intermediate (compass and map skills are required)

Portages: 2

Longest portage: 170 meters

Fee: No fee is required.

Alternative access:
McKinnon Road, off Highway 90, can be used to shorten the trip, but the road is usually flooded over in the spring and impossible to travel.

Alternative route:
The entire Willow Creek section can be paddled by putting in at Minesing Swamp Conservation Area parking lot, one kilometer south of the village of Minesing and ending at Edenvale Conservation Area on Highway 26.

Kayak friendly:
Only in high water levels

Outfitters: None

For more information:
NOTTAWASAGA VALLEY
CONSERVATION AUTHORITY
R.R. 1
Angus, Ontario
L0M 1B0
705-424-1479

Topographical maps:
Barrie 31 D/5

Beaver River

The lower section of the Beaver River is a fast and furious stretch of water, and come spring it can become a regular hangout for playboat enthusiasts. But in its upper reaches, between the hamlets of Kimberley and Heathcote, the hills of the deep, pre-glacial Beaver Valley flatten out, and the river calms into a gentle, more relaxing place.

The initial access point is along Grey County Road 13, just northeast of Kimberley. Look for a 100-metre-long bush road on the west side. The road leads down to a makeshift parking area alongside the river. This canoe launch was once maintained by the Ministry of Natural Resources, but the last time I used the site, I found the road full of potholes and the government sign dangling from a rotten fencepost. So be sure to keep a sharp eye out for the turnoff.

Before heading out, leave a second vehicle in Heathcote, on the left side and to the south of the county road bridge. Two side-road bridges west of County Road 13, just before Heathcote, also make for alternative take-out spots.

Remarkably, the four- or five-hour (20-kilometer) paddle remains wild well until the outskirts of Heathcote. In fact, because the banks of the Beaver River are composed mostly of silt and sand, and the top half meanders through a massive woodland swamp made up of silver maple and black ash, the poorly drained area was left abandoned by early inhabitants. The river was used only as a transportation route for the local natives, and then for a brief period between the 1840s and 1850s by settlers while they searched for new farmland. Eventually, the government decided to protect it and allow the public land to continue to provide habitat for waterfowl, white-tailed

Facing page: Members of the Durham Outdoor Club deal with another logjam along the Beaver River.

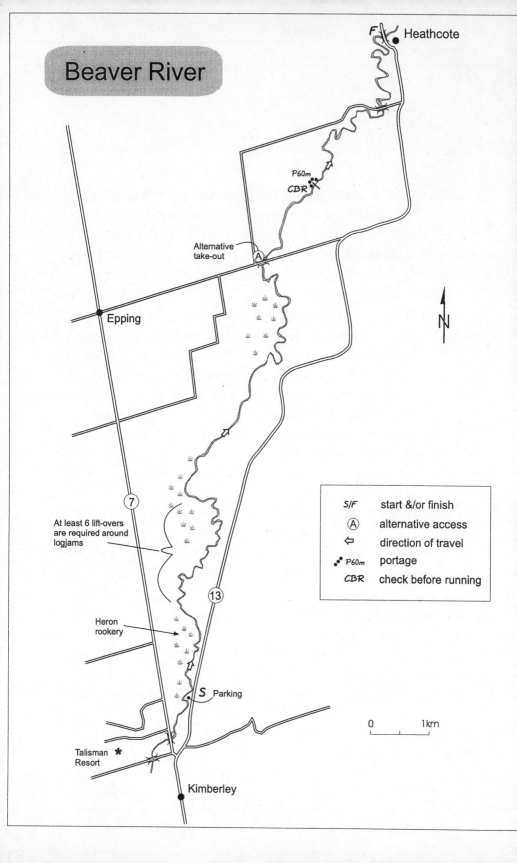

Beaver River

F — Heathcote

P60m
CBR

Alternative take-out — A

Epping

7

At least 6 lift-overs are required around logjams

13

Heron rookery

S Parking

Talisman Resort

Kimberley

S/F	start &/or finish
A	alternative access
⇐	direction of travel
P60m	portage
CBR	check before running

0   1km

N

Portaging through poison ivy and stinging nettle is the only real hazard along the Beaver River (Durham Outdoor Club).

deer, great blue herons (one of the largest rookeries in the area is located on the west bank, not far from the access point) and, of course, beaver.

The neighboring settlers once named the area Cuckoo Valley for the large number of black-billed cuckoos. But the original name, given by the Huron for the healthy population of beaver, has remained.

The water levels between Kimberley and Heathcote are good throughout the season, and the only sections of fast water to contend with are a few possible riffles at the put-in and a moderate swift approximately three-quarters the way along. The swift can be run easily. However, a 60-meter portage is marked on the left.

There are also at least half a dozen logjams clogging the first few kilometers of the route. Each has a short portage cleared on either the right or left bank, and the only real hazard is the poison ivy and stinging nettle growing along most of the pathways. Each logjam also provides an opportunity to fish for the rainbow and brown trout that make their way upstream by way of fish ladders constructed at the Thornbury and Clendenan dams.

It's not until just after the first of two county road bridges that cross the river south of Heathcote that the landscape opens up into farm pastures and housing developments. Here, you're more likely to spot a cow chewing its cud along the riverbank than an beaver gnawing away at a poplar tree — but it's an experience, just the same.

Beaver River

Time: 1 day (4 to 5 hours)

Difficulty: Novice

Portages:
7 (6 of them around logjams)

Longest portage: 60 meters

Fee:
Most of the Beaver River is on Crown land and no fee or permit is required.

Alternative access:
Two county road bridges just south of Heathcote can be used to shorten the route to a four-hour paddle.

Alternative route: None

Kayak friendly: Yes

Outfitters: None

For more information:
MINISTRY OF NATURAL RESOURCES
1450 Seventh Avenue East
Owen Sound, Ontario
N4K 2Z1
519-376-3860

GREY SAUBLE CONSERVATION AUTHORITY
R.R. 4
Owen Sound, Ontario
N4K 5N6
519-376-3076

Maps:
The Ministry of Natural Resources has produced a pamphlet, *Beaver River Canoe Route.*

Topographic Maps:
Markdale 41 A/7

Rankin and Sauble Rivers

I can not honestly say that I have always thought of Sauble Falls Provincial Park as a canoe destination. Most of my time spent there was in my youth, and back then the park was simply a place to pitch a tent while my friends and I hung around the beach all day. Recently, however, I returned to the park in late fall with my wife, Alana, and having little desire to build sandcastles or toss around a Frisbee on the frozen beach, we decided to go paddling instead.

The park offers two possible daytrips: an adventurous five-to-six-hour paddle down the Rankin River, or a more leisurely two-hour cruise up and then down the Sauble River. To organize a perfect paddling weekend, we chose to spend all day Saturday exploring the Rankin (rated the best river route on the Bruce Peninsula by some canoeists) and then leave half a day on Sunday to enjoy the unhurried pace of the Sauble with some friends of ours who live near Owen Sound.

My wife and I were lucky enough to book a waterfront site on the east side of the park and were able to use our tent spot as our take-out spot. However, if you can't reserve a site along the river, or simply haven't planned on staying overnight at the campground, a parking lot and launching area are available for both routes on the northwest side of the Highway 21 bridge.

To access the Rankin River route you have two choices. The first put-in is west of Highway 6. At the town of Mar, turn right off Highway 21 onto Red Bay Road, and use the launch site on the south side of the county road bridge that separates Sky Lake and Isaac Lake. If you don't wish to complete this full 18-kilometre section, choose choose a shorter route by accessing at Boat Lake Conservation Area on Bruce County Road 13.

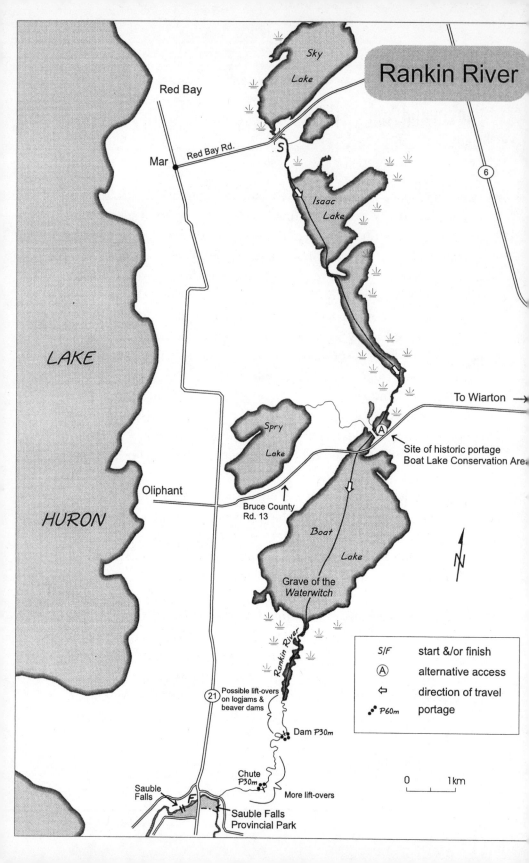

Alana and I chose to take on the full length of the route. Once we had convinced a gas station attendant working just north of the park to shuttle us up to the Red Bay Road launch site, we paddled south from the bridge. A one-kilometre narrow channel led us to the expanse of Isaac Lake, which is more of a gigantic wetland than an actual lake. The shoreline here is lined thick with marsh plants and in the distance, a collection of glacial drumlins are carpeted with birch and maple trees.

This mixture of hardwood forest and marshland makes for a prime breeding habitat for birds. In fact, the area holds a total of 125 resident species and is ranked the best overall birdwatching area on the Bruce Peninsula. Just in our paddle to the south end of Isaac Lake, Alana and I spotted buffleheads, mergansers, lesser and greater scaup, black terns, and marsh wrens. Among the dense reeds we also heard the distinct calls of the American bittern and both the Virginia and sora rail.

The passenger pigeon once made this area home as well. In the late 1800s, this was one of the largest passenger pigeon roosting areas in Southern Ontario, with an unbroken chain forming between the mouth of the Sauble River and inland and northward along Boat, Isaac, Sky, and Berford Lakes. The colony was so massive that the sound of them in flight was compared by one local settler to "the deep booming basso of the Canadian Falls at Niagara."

Many are the reasons given for the extinction of the passenger pigeon. It was most likely a mixture of over-harvesting and the bird's inability to adapt to an ever-changing environment. One sure thing is that the sheer volume of these birds made an everlasting impression. On the eve of their extinction in 1895, a Native chief, Simon Pokagon, gave this classic description of the vast flocks flying overhead: "I have seen them move in an unbroken column for hours across the sky, like some great river, ever varying in hue; and as the mighty stream sweeping on at sixty miles an hour, reached some deep valley, it would pour its living mass headlong down hundreds of feet, sounding as though a whirlwind was abroad in the land."

Steven and David Galloway counted forty-two turtles while out on the Sauble River.

The best way across Isaac Lake is to head directly south, keeping to the right-hand shoreline until eventually the lake narrows and then empties out into Boat Lake.

Two bridges cut across the weedy channel, connecting Isaac Lake with Boat Lake, and the county road that crosses over on the first bridge marks a portion of the historic Peninsula Portage. The trail, used by Native tribes for over two thousand years, was a shortcut to avoid the long and dangerous trip around the Bruce Peninsula. Heading inland from the present town of Wiarton on Georgian Bay, the portage ended here, at the southern tip of Isaac Lake. Then, the Natives would either continue overland to Spry Lake and then across the sand dunes to Lake Huron or head directly down the Rankin River and past Sauble Falls.

At the south end of Boat Lake lies another piece of history. Somewhere on the murky bottom lie the remains of the *Waterwitch*,

Sauble River

Legend:
- *S/F* — start &/or finish
- Ⓐ — alternative access
- ⇦ — direction of travel

Rankin River

Sauble Falls

S/F

Sauble Falls Provincial Park

21

Rapids

Ⓐ

Sauble Beach

Sauble River

Ⓐ

N

0   1km

8

a 12-meter steamer used on the river to move logs down to the mill at Sauble Falls up until the early 1890s. With the building of better roads in the area, however, the paddle wheeler quickly became obsolete and it was eventually sunk near the entrance to the Rankin.

The entrance to the river can be difficult to find at times, especially when high water spreads the river's banks out into the neighboring stands of silver maple. To avoid getting lost, just keep to the center of the flooded-out forest, and eventually the main current gives way to an obvious route choice. Other difficulties along the Rankin include a constant meander through dense forest and high sandy banks, which, combined with a strong current and a good number of blow-downs lying across the stream, can call for some quick maneuvering at times. Two portages are also necessary en route before the Rankin River meets up with the larger Sauble River. The first is a 30-metre trail to the left of a concrete dam constructed by the conservation authority back in 1961 and the second is another 30-metre trail (marked to the right) avoiding a dangerous chute located just beyond a sharp bend in the river.

The Rankin River continues its fast pace, cutting through sand dunes and over the odd beaver dam and jumble of logs, right to where it flows under the county road bridge and the confluence of the Sauble River. From here, it's a mere twenty-minute paddle downriver to reach the campground.

Even though Alana and I enjoyed the challenges of the Rankin River, the next day on the Sauble provided a much better route for our friends from Owen Sound. Doug Galloway, who has traveled with me on countless adventures in Algonquin, was used to canoe travel. But for his wife, Kim, and two sons, David and Steven, this would be their first time in a canoe. The slow-moving current of the Sauble River, and its scenic shoreline, free of any cottage or housing development, made for a perfect day outing.

The plan for the day was simply to paddle up the Sauble until we could go no further — there are three sets of swifts just downstream from the first county road bridge. Ours was a leisurely pace, to say the least, and it took only three hours to complete the full route. But for the novices of the group, it was a full day's adventure, following every twist and turn of the river as it carved its way through tall sand dunes, marking the remnants of the 10,000-year-old sand plains laid down by Lake Algonquin. And like other rivers running through the farmland of Bruce County, the Sauble also provided an excellent place to spot wildlife. By the end of the day, David and Steven had counted a total of forty-two turtles sunning themselves on half-submerged logs, five Chinook salmon swimming upstream to spawn, and two white-tailed deer peering down at us from a thick plantation of red pine. It was a wonderful day, and we were even able to end it off by driving to the town of Sauble Beach for a double scoop of ice cream before heading for home — now, that's a canoe trip!

Rankin and Sauble Rivers

Time: 1 day (2 to 5 hours)

Difficulty:
Some paddling experience is needed for the Rankin River, especially during high water levels, but the Sauble River is a perfect novice route.

Portages:
The Rankin River has only two and the Sauble River has none.

Longest portage: 30 meters

Fee:
A camping permit is required if you wish to stay over at Sauble Falls Provincial Park, and there is a parking fee at the take-outs for both the Rankin River and Sauble River routes.

Alternative access:
Boat Lake Conservation Area, located along Bruce County Road 13, can be used as an alternative access for the Rankin River route, and the Sauble River route can be extended by shuttling a vehicle to one of a number of side-road bridges off Highway 8.

Alternative route:
The Sauble River route can be extended by putting in upstream on a number of side-road bridges.

Kayak friendly:

The Sauble River route is suited for kayaks but the Rankin River is best in open canoes.

Outfitters:

THORNCREST OUTFITTERS
193 High Street
Southhampton, Ontario
N0H 2L0
519-797-1608

COWAN CANOES AND
KAYAK LIVERY
316 Mill Street
Paisley, Ontario
N0G 2N0
519-353-5535

THE GREATER SAUGEEN
TRADING CO.
473 Queen Street
Paisley, Ontario

N0G 2N0
519-353-4453

For more information:

MINISTRY OF NATURAL
RESOURCES
Owen Sound District Office
1450 Seventh Avenue East
Owen Sound, Ontario
N4K 2Z1
519-376-3860

SAUBLE FALLS
PROVINCIAL PARK
R.R. 3
Wiarton, Ontario
N0H 2T0
519-422-1952
1-888-668-7275 (for reservations)

Topographical maps:

Wiarton 41 A/11

Both the Rankin and Sauble Rivers make perfect family outings.

Noganosh Lake

I'm always on the lookout for that unsung canoe route — some obscure river or lake that other paddlers seem to know little about. A secret spot that has miraculously remained undeveloped, even wild. Then, after spending hours glancing over maps, reading guide-books, browsing the Web, and then heading out and "testing the waters," I most likely will find the portages overgrown, water levels unnavigable, and the shoreline taken over by private ownership. On that rare occasion, however, I manage to hit the jackpot. An obscure route with short portages, pristine campsites, and unbelievable fishing. A place like Noganosh Lake.

Alana and I, along with our hyper springer spaniel, Bailey, discovered this route in late August 1999. I had just got back from a lengthy trip in Wabakimi — a wilderness park 300 kilometers north of Thunder Bay — and Alana was a little jealous that her summer canoeing was only a few weekend jaunts to busy recreational parks in the south. Of course, the size of the Noganosh area couldn't come close to Wabikimi's vast 100,000 hectares of remote boreal forest. But the feeling of remoteness was pretty darn close at times.

We used the Ess Narrows access point on the northeast side of the Highway 522, 21 kilometers west of the town of Loring. From here, we paddled under the highway bridge and began the long 3-kilometer paddle down the length of Dollars Lake to Kawigamog Lake (named after the steamboat that worked the area lakes in the early 1900s). This is the most boring section en route, especially with the dozens of cottages dotting the shoreline and heavy motorboat traffic racing down the waterway. Alana and I made the best of it, waving at each cottager sitting on their dock and gesturing a thank-you to all the passing boats that slowed down to reduce their wake.

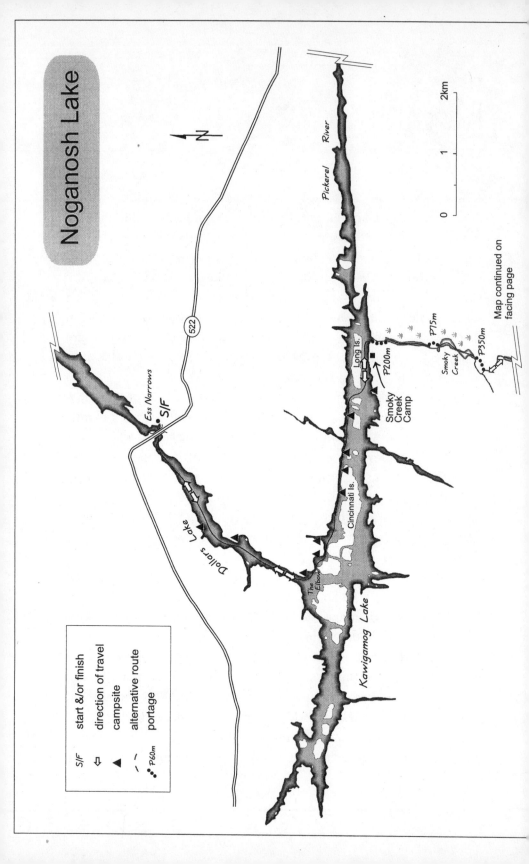

Noganosh Lake

S/F — start &/or finish
⇦ — direction of travel
▲ — campsite
– – – — alternative route
•••• P60m — portage

522

Ess Narrows
S/F

Dollars Lake

The Elbow

Kawigamog Lake

Cincinnati Is.

Long Is.

Pickerel River

P200m
Smoky Creek Camp
P75m
Smoky Creek
P350m

Map continued on facing page

0   1   2km

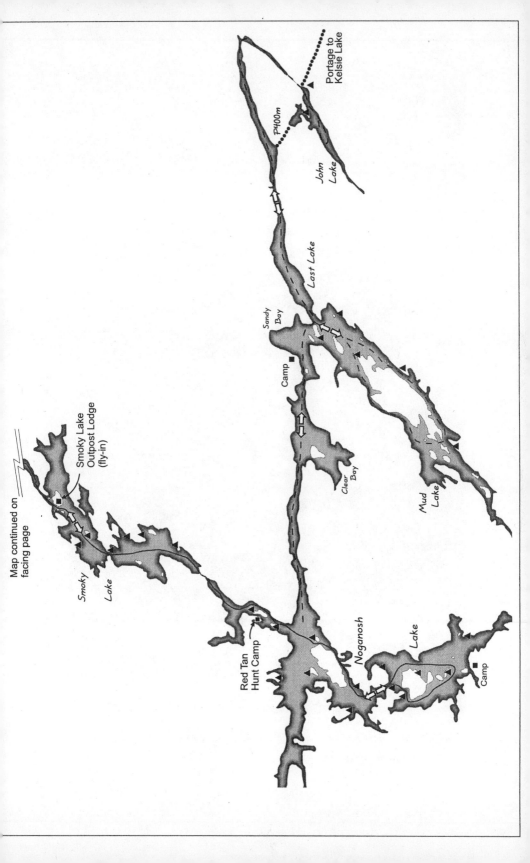

Map continued on facing page

Smoky Lake Outpost Lodge (fly-in)

Smoky Lake

Red Tan Hunt Camp

Noganosh Lake

Camp

Clear Bay

Camp

Sandy Bay

Mud Lake

Last Lake

John Lake

P400m

Portage to Kelsie Lake

Smoky Lake is just one of the five connecting lakes on the Noganosh route waiting to be explored.

Actually, in slowing down, the chop increases, but it's the thought that counts.

Once at the junction of Dollars Lake and Kawigamog Lake, we took the more isolated channel along the north side of the Elbow and Cincinnati Island rather than heading straight out to the center of the lake. There's no cottage development here and little boat traffic. There are even a number of makeshift campsites that have been developed on Crown land for canoeists who arrive late in the day and need a place to stay before heading all the way into the Noganosh area. Be warned, however, that these sites become party central on a long weekend.

Approximately 2 kilometers east, the out-of-the-way channel, now called the Pickerel River, opens up. After reaching the west side of Long Island, Alana and I slowly made our way across to the south shore to search for the outlet of Smoky Creek and the first of three portages.

Eventually we located the take-out between the Smoky Creek Hunt Camp and the creek itself. It's a clear, 200-meter trail, chewed up by constant ATV use coming out of the hunt club, and it avoids a giant beaver dam that keeps the water level on Smoky Creek navigable throughout the season. Even in high water, though, the next 2 kilometers of upstream paddling to reach the next portage — a 75-meter path heading up and over a steep knoll to the left of another large beaver dam — can be extremely frustrating. Countless times the creek snakes back on itself, and by the end you've covered more than three times the distance.

You can see the third and final portage from the put-in of the last 75-meter lift-over. It looks straightforward from here, with a weed-choked passageway meandering through to the west. But Alana and I found ourselves at the end of at least two dead-end channels before we finally pulled up at the proper take-out to the left of the creek.

The trail was the longest en route — measuring a little over 300 meters — but it was relatively flat and straightforward. About a quarter of the way along, however, we took some time out to follow a side trail across from where a weathered sign was nailed to a pine tree to commemorate a local hunter who was killed in the area. The path crossed the creek and made its way slowly up a winding hill toward the remains of an old broken-down pickup. A wide assortment of rusted trucks and dilapidated hunt camps can be found throughout the area, reminders of how well traveled the region has been throughout the years, mostly due to the abundance of deer. To this day, this section of forested land south of Lake Nippissing holds the largest gathering of white-tailed deer in the province. Known as the Loring herd, it consists of eight to fourteen thousand individuals.

After the last portage, the creek runs directly south for half a kilometer, snakes around to the west, and then opens up into Smoky Lake. Here, on an island, is Smoky Lake Lodge, a fly-in camp owned by Tornados Outfitting. It's mostly American fishermen who come here to try their luck for a trophy smallmouth bass or monster pike. When Alana and I passed the docks of the camp, we said hello to some of the occupants sitting out on the main porch. I guess after spending a good bit of cash to be flown into the remote lake, they were all a little taken aback, witnessing our leisurely paddle in on our own. One of the customers, an elderly man dressed in full Elmer Fudd costume, yelled out to us, "How the hell did y'all get into this godforsaken lake?" Not wanting to ruin his "wilderness experience," we babbled some crazed story of spending hours on muddy portages and bug-infested swamps. It was an outright lie, but the man felt sorry enough for us that he handed Alana and me each a beer before we headed down the lake to make camp.

Our choice of sites was a secluded spot, tucked into a back bay on the southeast end of Smoky Lake. Noganosh Lake itself has far more ideal places to camp but I caught a four-pound bass while drifting by the spot on Smoky Lake and quickly decided it would be a good place to stay.

The next day, Alana, Bailey and I headed out early to explore, not only Noganosh Lake, but also three other connecting lakes (Last Lake, John Lake and Mud Lake). Ideally, it would have been best to bring along our camp gear and stay overnight on a second site.

There's so much open water to explore here, with the remains of a ranger station and firetower to search for in the bush along the north shore of the western inlet and a scattering of islands across the southern bay offering perfect spots for a shore lunch, that you could spend an entire week on Noganosh Lake alone. But Alana and I had only planned a quick weekend getaway for this trip and, with it being the summer solstice, we decided to take advantage of the extended light of the longest day of the year and explore as much to the east as possible.

In the early morning calm, we quickly paddled through the shallow channel joining Smoky Lake with Noganosh Lake, slowed down only to check out a couple of rustic hunt camps, and then made haste down the long eastern inlet toward the first adjoining lake.

The channel remained unaltered all the way to the entrance to Clear Bay, Sandy Bay and then Last Lake (all great places to troll for bass or pike). We kept to the north shore for most of the route, staying close to the massive outcropping of rock that would block the wind and made for easy paddling.

By midday we found ourselves roaming the lower portion of Mud Lake, and we stopped for lunch at a makeshift campsite. It was an unappealing site, cluttered with tin cans, cigarette butts and a giant sheet of plastic tied to four dead birch trees. Even the landscape around it didn't compare well with the Algonquin-like character of our base camp on Smoky. I did manage, however, to hook into a trophy bass that jumped seven times and tugged on my line for twenty minutes before it finally broke free.

It was getting quite late by the time we circled around back to the top of Last Lake. So we chose to leave John Lake, located more than 4 kilometers further east, for another trip. It was a good call. By the time we got back to our base camp on Smoky, it was getting dark and we had to resort to a quick dinner of macaroni and cheese before heading off to bed.

By late morning the next day we managed to crawl out of our tent and start packing up to go home. Even poor Bailey, who I don't recall paddling a single stroke the day before, was totally exhausted and was quite slow taking in her morning routine — a leisurely swim and a game of tag with the camp chipmunk.

On our return trip we stopped to say hello to the Elmer Fudd look-a-like who was fishing at the entrance to Smoky Creek. Alana and I pulled alongside his aluminum fishing boat and asked the age-old question "Having any luck?" The American simply smirked and reported he had caught nothing all morning — even though I caught a glimpse of a full stringer of fish dangling off the back side of his boat. I kept quiet about his catch, thinking he was just an average angler who was trying to keep his newly found fishing hole a secret (something I totally respect). Either that or he was just feeling sorry for two canoeists who had to the deal with hours of battling bugs and muddy portages while he waited comfortably for a plane to pick him up at the end of the day.

We wished him a pleasant flight and he wished us good luck on the portages, neither of us knowing that we would all meet again that same day. It was the craziest thing. After Alana and I padded back out to the Ess Narrows access point and headed down the highway for home, we stopped at the local coffee shop in the town of Loring. There, sitting at the counter, was the American fisherman. At first, he didn't quite recognize us. After all, we had him believing that the trip out of Smoky Lake was a painstaking ordeal that would take us at least a full day, not a three-hour pleasure cruise. But then he heard our dog Bailey barking at us to get a move on, and it finally dawned on him who Alana and I were. "My God!" he said "How the hell did you get back so soon?"

There was nothing I could do but lie again. This time it was a doozie. I told him that we had actually met a bush pilot in the next lake and paid him for a quick lift back to Loring. Thinking about it, the fib wasn't all that terrible a thing to do. After all, in the end, the American's concept of wilderness was left intact and our easy and inexpensive paddle route into the Noganosh system was kept a secret — unless he reads this book, that is.

Noganosh Lake

Difficulty:
Since this is an unmaintained route, moderate tripping experience is recommended.

Portages:
6 (3 that have to be doubled back on)

Longest portage: 300 meters

Fee:
This is an unmaintained provincial park and no fee is required.

Alternative access:
Tornados outpost camp provides a fly-in service to their lodge on Smoky Lake.

Alternative route:
The Ministry of Natural Resources is now considering working on some old portages that were once used to connect this route with the Magnetawan River to the south.

Kayak friendly:
Yes (use a cart for the portages)

Outfitters:
GRUNDY LAKE SUPPLY POST
R.R. 1
Highway 69 & Highway 522
Britt, Ontario
P0G 1A0
705-383-2251

For more information:
MINISTRY OF NATURAL RESOURCES
Parry Sound District Office
7 Bay Street
Parry Sound, Ontario
705-746-4201

TORNADOS CANADIAN RESORTS
c/o Ralf and Christine Strub
Box 26
Port Loring, Ontario
P0H 1Y0
800-663-2277
705-757-2050

Topographical maps:
Noganosh 41 H/16

Big East Lake

For ten years now I've worked as a part-time Environmental Issues instructor at Sir Sandford Fleming College in Lindsay, Ontario. The course mostly deals with human overpopulation, pollution, resource extraction, the lack of biodiversity, and even the fallacy of conservation. Basically it's a general outlook on our high-handed, superior views toward nature, and quite honestly the job gets darn depressing at times.

A few years back — after weeks of lecturing on toxic spills, clear cutting, the extinction of species — I had to give my students some encouragement, a little dash of hope. So I handed out an assignment where they had to research a "good news" case study, something that was a positive approach toward caring for our environment. A week later they gathered into the lecture hall, handed me their papers, and firmly stated that it was the most difficult assignment I had ever given them. Not for the marking scheme itself — I'm one of the less demanding professors at the college — but the fact that each student found nothing other than a handful of band-aid solutions.

Imagine my dilemma. I had to mark all these daunting case studies and, for the students' sake, still remain optimistic. Realizing that the best place to gain a positive outlook toward nature was nature itself, I packed up my canoe gear immediately after class and headed north to Haliburton's Big East Lake. The lake, situated directly across from the more popular Poker Lake loop, is a perfect quick fix for canoeists (or depressed environmental issues instructors looking to re-energize themselves).

Facing page: Haliburton's Big East Lake provides a quick fix for any weekend canoeist.

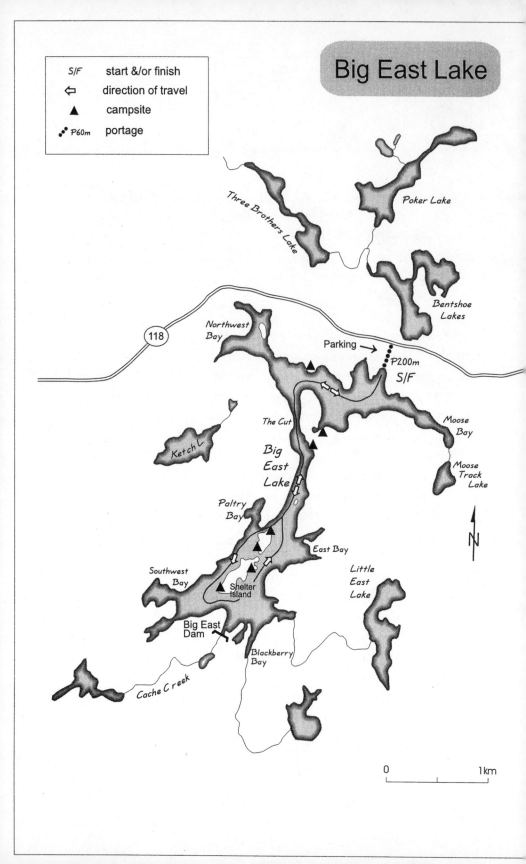

Bailey — the runt of the litter but a perfect canoe dog.

It was a good two-hour drive to the parking area on the south side of Highway 118, 20 kilometers west of Highway 35, and another twenty minutes to double carry my canoe and pack down the 200-meter trail to the launch site. By the time I paddled to the far southwest end of the lake to make camp on a large island, carpeted with a good stand of pine and white birch, I just had enough light to erect my tent and gather a bundle of firewood.

After a quick dinner, I brewed up a large pot of tea, and by the dim light of the campfire, I marked papers well into the night.

I was a little late for my nine o'clock class the next day. But when I finally wandered into the lecture hall to meet my students, offering excuses for my tardiness and the pungent smell of smoke coming off my clothes, the news that I had their papers already marked and that each student had received a passing grade helped erase any ill feelings. With an upbeat attitude, I continued to lecture that day, talking about the pleasures of wild places and the willingness most of us have to protect the familiar, once we become familiar with it. And to this day I make an annual pilgrimage back to Big East Lake, not with students' assignments but rather with the students themselves. In fact, an overnight canoe trip to Big East Lake has become a prerequisite for my course. It's a tad more work than simply marking essays but I think it's a far more effective teaching tool.

Big East Lake

Time: 2 days

Difficulty: Novice

Portages:
One (the trail leading down to the canoe launch)

Longest portage: 200 meters

Fee:
Big East Lake is situated on Crown land and no fee is required for Canadian citizens.

Alternative access: No

Alternative route:
The Poker Lake Loop (described in my book *Cottage Country Canoe Routes*) is a two-day loop accessed directly across from the Big East parking lot and makes an excellent side trip.

Kayak friendly: Yes

Outfitters: None

For more information:
MINISTRY OF NATURAL RESOURCES
Minden District Office
Box 820
Minden, Ontario
K0M 2K0
705-286-1521

Maps:
A good reference is the *Poker Lake Adventure Map* produced by Chrismar Mapping Service.

Topographical maps:
Haliburton 31 E/2

Silent Lake Provincial Park

If you ask any canoeists to list the one piece of equipment that they have always cherished, you'll most likely find that their most-prized personal possessions share one crucial element — tradition! Never will their lists include a high-priced Gortex jacket, a technologically advanced GPS (Global Positioning System), or a sleek, new-age Kevlar boat. Rather, the list will include either a leaky rubberized slicker, a not-so-accurate brass-plated compass or, most likely, a water-logged canvas-covered canoe. There's no real logic or sound defense for using such ancient items. Most modern-day merchandise far exceeds the gear of the past performance-wise. But there is one thing that Gortex, nylon, plastic and Kevlar don't have, and that's soul.

This deep reverence for the past, especially when it comes to wooden canoes, is particularly strong in Peterborough — the birth-place of the modern-day canoe and my home for the past dozen years. I quickly realized the city's strong canoe culture when I went to my first local canoe club meeting. I was equipped with a brand-new 18-foot Kevlar canoe weighing a mere 42 pounds. The other members, all outfitted with wood and canvas models, gave it a quick look, nicknamed it "The Potato Chip," and throughout the meeting, in a very serious manner, I might add, repeatedly asked when I was going to get a "real" canoe.

It wasn't until five years later that my wife and I received a 1954 Peterborough wood and canvas canoe as a wedding gift from some friends. It was rotten at both ends and was sinfully covered in fiber-glass, and it took me another two years to restore it, but eventually it became an approved model by all the members of the club.

I'll never forget the day I first paddled it. It was early spring and the last coating of pale-blue paint I had given the canvas was finally dry. I had chosen the color blue for the same reason that Canadian

artist Tom Thomson had — so the trout swimming underneath couldn't spot me passing over them.

In doing so, I had to choose a fitting route. It had to be a place full of heritage, a waterway free of any motorboats or cottage lots, and, most important, the lake itself had to contain plenty of trout to sneak up on.

Silent Lake Provincial Park, situated just off Highway 28, 21 kilometres north of Apsley and less than an hour's drive from my home in Peterborough, was perfect. This 1,420-hectare Natural Environment Park is like a miniature Algonquin, hosting a single lake where motorized boats are prohibited; the only development is the main campground tucked away in a forest of second-growth pine, maple and oak; and lake trout are stocked on a regular basis.

The land was previously owned by Six Point Lodge, built by an American company in 1927, and was later purchased by the Crown in 1967, with the park being officially opened in 1975.

The campground offers a choice of 167 main sites, a small collection of remote walk-in sites, and a fourteen-person lodge and six-person yurt (a fabric-covered shelter with a wooden platform) for organized groups or clubs. All of these can provide an enjoyable camping experience.

Silent Lake can be accessed by a total of three launch areas — two in the campground and one in the day-use area — and for the most part, canoeists spend the day just circling the lake. At the far end of the eastern inlet, however, three smaller interconnecting lakes (Quiet Lake, Soft Lake and Hush Lake) present an even more remote place to paddle. Take note, however, that during low water levels, the lakes become choked with weeds and can be difficult to navigate through. And of the three portages that link them together, only the first (an 80-meter trail to the right of the creek that drains out of Quiet Lake) actually resembles a proper portage. The remain-

Facing page: Silent Lake Provincial Park is a miniature Algonquin, hosting a single lake where motorized boats are prohibited.

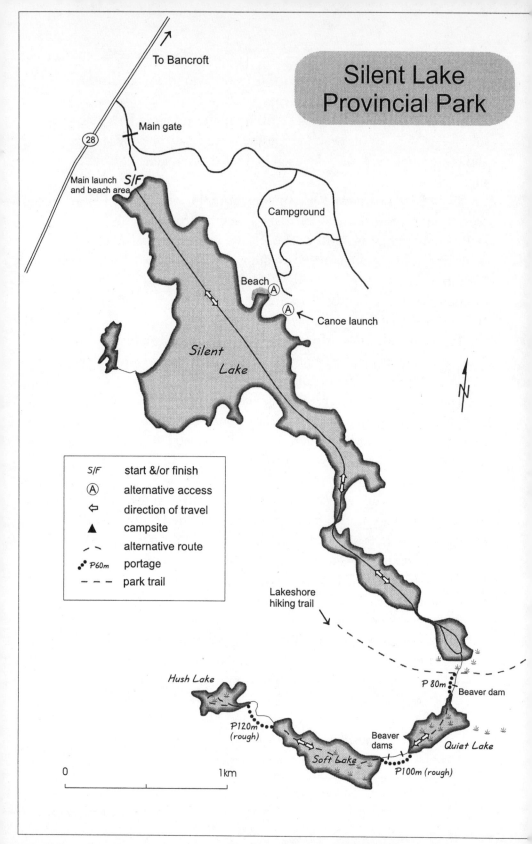

Quiet Lake, reached by a short portage from Silent Lake's eastern inlet, offers an even more remote place to paddle.

ing two are just bush trails found on the left of a dried-up creek. The paths measure 100 meters and 120 meters in length and lead you precariously up and over a steep knob of granite.

I remember the almost non-existent portages well. In fact, I cursed the weight of my newly restored canoe and wished I had brought my lightweight Kevlar model along instead. I even managed to scratch off so much pale-blue paint from all the half-submerged rocks piled up at the put-ins and take-outs that I failed to sneak up on a single lake trout while making my way back. I must admit, though, that it was a wonderful canoe to paddle. It had both intitial and secondary stability and was far more responsive than any other canoe I've tried. Even more important, the boat definitely had soul, and by the end of the day I was totally in love with it. So much so, that of the six canoes I now own, my pale-blue wood-and-canvas canoe is always the first to be unloaded from the storage shed at the beginning of the season and taken out for a paddle — preferably on Silent Lake, of course.

Silent Lake Provincial Park

Difficulty:
Novice

Portages:
3 (only necessary if you wish to explore the three connecting ponds)

Longest portage: 120 meters

Fee:
An overnight camping permit is required (reservations are recommended).

Alternative access:
There are three possible launch areas — two in the campground and one at the day-use area.

Alternative route:
A side trip can be taken to three connecting lakes (Quiet Lake, Soft Lake, Hush Lake) located at the far end of Silent Lake's eastern inlet.

Kayak friendly: Yes

Outfitters:
The main campground offers canoe rentals.

For more information:
SILENT LAKE PROVINCIAL PARK
Box 500
Bancroft, Ontario
K0L 1C0
613-339-2807
For reservations call
1-888-668-7275

Topographical maps:
Gooderham 31 D/16

Crab Lake

Noel's requests were quite demanding for his son's first canoe trip. He wanted a quick and easy route only a couple of hours drive from his home near Guelph; maybe a short portage so five-year-old Walker could experience, for a brief moment, what it felt to shoulder all your belongings on your back; and a choice campsite set on a remote lake that happens to be populated by monster-sized bass. Noel (the editor for my publishing company) had been on a number of trips with me before and I knew he wouldn't be at all surprised to hear that such a perfect trip didn't exist. But it did. A place called Crab Lake. And it's a gem I couldn't wait to share with him and Walker.

Crab Lake can be reached by Wolf Lake, which has an access point on its far eastern end. To reach the launch site, turn left off Highway 28, just south of Apsley, and onto Anstruther Lake Road. Then, exactly 5 kilometers along, an unmarked dirt road to the left will lead you down to Wolf Lake. It seems like a relatively easy process, but because the last road is not marked, you can easily find yourself lost. Our group missed the turn for Wolf Lake twice and even somehow managed to begin paddling across a totally different lake for half an hour before we realized our mistake. We then resorted to asking a local cottager to steer us in the right direction.

Wolf Lake is a perfect destination on its own. Only a few cottages crowd the lake, mostly along the south shore, and a strip of Crown land along the north shore, as well as a number of small islands to the west, provide some excellent campsite possibilities. Crab Lake is much more isolated, however, and is easily reached by way of a short, 107-meter portage. The take-out is located at the far end of Wolf Lake's southwest bay, just before the last two cottages along the south shore.

"This is how ya catch fish, Dad" (Walker "Bass Master" Hudson, Crab Lake).

Crab Lake has five main bays that head off in all directions (therefore its local name, Star Lake) and it is much larger than it first appears. Each inlet also has one or two prime campsites, complete with an exposed chunk of granite to catch a breeze on to escape the bugs and a snug canopy of pine, maple and birch to pitch a tent under. Our group chose an out-of-the way spot directly below where a rough trail heads up to the top of Blueberry Mountain (an exposed hill that's literally covered in thick blueberry bushes) and after quickly setting up camp, we headed out in the canoe again in search of the lake's monster bass.

We cast our lines out the moment we entered the first weedy bay; Noel and I with our fancy plugs and spinners, and Walker with his half-dead worm stuck on a bear hook. It was my idea to give Walker the defunct bait, thinking the lake's healthy population of sunfish would keep him occupied at least long enough for Noel and me to catch some decent-sized bass for supper. Of course, in no time at all, Walker had caught three bass, averaging around four pounds each, and Noel and I hadn't even had a single bite. Quickly we switched to the decomposing worms and, in exchange, allowed Walker free rein on our lure boxes. Ten minutes later Walker had caught two more trophy bass (one on my scent-impregnated rubber frog and the other on Noel's pink-coloured "Holla-Popper"). Noel and I still remained fishless.

I doubt that this lake had ever given up so many fish. In fact, Noel and I were quite mystified by Walker's success and had to blame it on beginner's luck to settle our egos. Walker, on the other hand, had a different reason for catching so many lunkers. Each time he lowered his line into the water, the intrepid angler would whisper a secret code — "Here fishy, fishy, fishy." Walker was insistent that without saying this magical phrase, no fish would ever bite the hook. So, we agreed to play along for the fun of it — or maybe we were just that desperate to catch a fish — and both tossed out our lines and repeated the expression "Here fishy, fishy, fishy." Ten minutes later Noel and I had caught a couple of bass each.

Legend

S/F	start &/or finish
⇦	direction of travel
▲	campsite
•‌•‌• *P60m*	portage

Crab Lake

To Hwy. 28

Anstruther Lake Rd.

S/F

Wolf Lake

P107m

Crab Lake

N

Blueberry Mountain (Sharpe's Rock)

0   1km

A perfect morning on a perfect lake (Crab Lake's southeast bay).

Thinking back, the trip to Crab Lake wasn't a complete success, not according to Noel's set criteria. The route was actually two-and-a-half hours' drive from his home; Walker only carried his personal pack halfway along the portage before handing it over to his father; and Noel and I never did catch a trophy bass. It did manage to fulfill his main objective, though — Walker can't wait until next year's trip — and according to Noel, a father can't ask for anything more perfect than that.

Crab Lake

Difficulty: Novice

Portages: 1

Longest portage: 107 meters

Fee:
Crab Lake is an unmaintained provincial park and no fee is required.

Alternative access: None

Alternative route:
Some canoeists prefer to stay on one of the Crown land sites on Wolf Lake.

Kayak friendly: Yes

Outfitters:
WILD ROCK OUTFITTERS
169 Charlotte Street
Peterborough, Ontario
K9J 2T7
705-745-9133

ADVENTURE FITNESS
Buckhorn Road & County Road 18
R.R. 3
Lakefield, Ontario
K0L 2H0
705-652-7986

For more information:
MINISTRY OF NATURAL RESOURCES
Bancroft District Office
Box 500
Bancroft, Ontario
K0L 1C0
613-332-3940

Topographical maps:
Burleigh Falls 31 D/9

Wolf Island Provincial Park

I was twelve when my father took me on my very first canoe trip. Actually, it wasn't a true canoe trip. We were staying at a fly-in fishing lodge — something we did every summer — and spent a good part of the week trolling the main lake without much luck. By the second-last day, my father and I decided to borrow one of the lodge's beat-up aluminum canoes and portage into a neighboring lake and try for speckle trout. Boy, did we catch fish.

To this day, I have always preferred the canoe over the convenience of the outboard motor. My father, however, hasn't been in one since — that is, until last year's fishing trip to Wolf Island.

The island is a relatively unknown provincial park situated along the Trent-Severn Waterway, between Lovesick Lake and Lower Buckhorn Lake. It was originally designated a Natural Environment Park for its unique geological features, where Paleozoic limestone outcroppings rub shoulders with much older Precambrian bedrock. A number of crescent-shaped gouges and striations were marked deep in the bedrock by the passing glaciers, and the mixture of swamp forest and barren rockscape makes for an interesting habitat.

There's no road access directly to Wolf Island, so my father and I chose to head out from the parking lot and boat launch at the Burleigh Falls Lock, and paddle west to reach the park. The conventional lock, one of thirty-six found along the 386-kilometer Trent-Severn Waterway and managed by Parks Canada, is located just north of the falls and on the left side of Highway 28.

It took us well over an hour to navigate through a dozen or so tiny islands, and then across an exposed stretch of Lovesick Lake before reaching Wolf Island.

It was a relaxed paddle, though. The clouds were high and the leftover mist from the night before still clung to the water's surface,

All things considered, my father took the dunking quite well (Trent Severn Waterway's Wolf Island Provincial Park).

making for an incredible calm. We even stopped twice along the way to pour coffee from our Thermos and make a couple of casts for walleye or possibly a muskie.

Once at Wolf Island's east shore, our plan was to spend the rest of the day circling it counterclockwise. The island, as well as some of the small surrounding islands, has designated campsites. (Take note that some islands to the west are owned by Curve Lake Indian Reserve; please respect their private land.) It's also a non-operating park and the campsites are free of charge. But I hadn't planned on us staying the night. Heck, it was hard enough to convince my father to sit in a canoe all day, let alone sleep on the cold ground.

To get to the opposite side of the island, there's portages around four dams (Sunrise, Sunset, Black Duck and Grey Duck), an old abandoned canoe lift-over, and the Lovesick Lock. Our choice was a 60-meter trail around the north side of Grey Duck Dam, the second of the two dams to the north.

Between the towns of Kimberley and Heathcote, the Beaver River remains remarkably wild, meandering through massive woodland swamps of silver maple and black ash.

Top: The "Crash-Test Dummies" (John and Kathy) minutes before they dumped in mid-rapid and somehow managed to wrap my favorite boat around a large boulder. Bottom: Enticed by a promise of honey ahead, Pooh steels himself for a ride through the rapids on Grants Creek. But he just can't bear to look…

Top: Grants Creek constantly varies, from almost stagnant water to a series of impressive drops. Bottom: While paddling the Noganosh route, Alana and I found a perfect campsite tucked into a back bay on the southeast end of Smoky Lake.

Facing page: Preparing cinnamon rolls on a paddle.
This page: The Harkin gang (Jim, Keelan and Ryan)
practice paddling techniques before embarking on the
historic Thames River, only three blocks from their home
in London.

Top: Another scenic cascade along the Grants Creek canoe route.
Bottom: Joeperry Lake is a relatively isolated place with plenty of
prime campsites and a giant beach that extends all the way along the
northeast shoreline.

Top: "At least it's bigger than the one you caught, Dad." Walker "Bass Master" Hudson strikes again while fishing on Crab Lake.
Bottom: Lost again in Minesing Swamp.

Time for a coffee break along the Nonquon River.

A maze of small islands and rocky shoals surrounding Wolf Island Provincial Park help keep the boat traffic to a minimum.

After a few minutes of pushing through thick weed beds and finding ourselves lost at the end of two dead-end bays, we found the proper take-out below the dam and began carrying our canoe and gear over the portage.

Things were going great so far. I managed to catch a few perch below the dam and my father managed to avoid all the poison ivy growing thick along the trail. (He's had a terrible reaction to it since using it as toilet paper years ago.) Then, after successfully loading up the canoe without any mishap, everything went downhill. With my father positioned in the front seat, I pushed us off from shore, tripped on an exposed root, and tipped the canoe. In seconds, gallons of water poured in and before we could register what had happened, my father and I were both swimming in a mixture of water and swamp ooze.

All things considered, my dad took the dunking quite well. He only cursed a bit and then slowly made his way to shore, while leaving

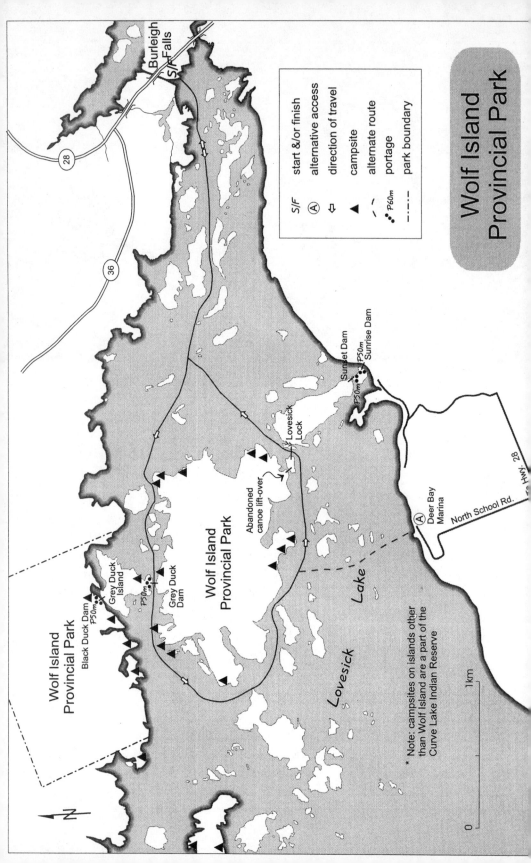

Wolf Island
Provincial Park

Legend

S/F	start &/or finish
Ⓐ	alternative access
⇧	direction of travel
▲	campsite
⌒	alternate route
•••• P60m	portage
—··—	park boundary

Burleigh
S/F Falls

28

36

Wolf Island
Provincial Park

Black Duck Dam
P50m

Grey Duck
Island
P50m

Grey Duck
Dam

Wolf Island
Provincial Park

Abandoned
canoe lift-over

Lovesick
Lock

Sunset Dam
P50m
P50m
Sunrise Dam

Deer Bay
Marina

North School Rd.

HWY. 28

Lovesick Lake

* Note: campsites on islands other
than Wolf Island are a part of the
Curve Lake Indian Reserve

N

0   1km

me to fish out our gear and bail out the canoe. The truth is, I thought for sure he'd call it quits right then and there. Surprisingly, though, he just poured us a third cup of coffee and then motioned for us to continue.

By noon our clothes had nearly dried out and we had caught enough perch to enjoy a shore lunch on one of the designated campsites. To get back over to Lovesick Lake, we both decided that a ride on the Lovesick Lock was a better option than portaging around another dam.

We spotted the lock station the moment we reached the south end of the island. The gatehouses along the Trent-Severn system are pretty much identical — painted brown and yellow with a perfectly manicured lawn. As we approached the lock, the huge metal gates were left open, as if the lockmaster knew of our intentions, and we paddled directly into the chamber.

My dad held the canoe steady alongside the mossy concrete wall while I got out and paid the moderate fee for passage. (The charge is by the length of the vessel.) I must admit that when I returned to the canoe, our boat looked a little silly floating alongside expensive yachts and the assortment of pleasure craft. They all appeared to tower over us and each crew member seemed to be giving us a strange look, as if we didn't belong. The lockmaster waited for one more cruiser to fill the chamber and then began cranking a wheel to close the back doors. Soon we heard a gurgling noise and the water level began to drop. Lovesick Lock is the smallest in the system and we only dropped down a meter, which is nothing if you consider that the entire system from the Summit at Balsam Lake to the Bay of Quinte drops down 182 meters. It's an enjoyable ride just the same.

Eventually the doors in front of us opened up and all the boats emptied out of the chamber in an orderly fashion. The whole process took about ten to fifteen minutes, and it would have been faster to portage. But we did manage to keep dry through the whole ordeal.

Wolf Island Provincial Park

Difficulty: Novice

Portages: 2

Longest portage: 60 meters

Fee:
This is an unmaintained provincial park and no camping fee is required, but you have to pay for parking at the Burleigh Falls Lock or the alternative access at Deer Bay Marina.

Alternative access:
Deer Bay Marina can be used as a way to avoid any portaging. Reach the marina by turning left off Highway 28 (just north of Young's Point) and onto North School Road. It's approximately 7 kilometers to the marina.

Alternative route:
Using Deer Bay Marina as an alternative access, you can simply paddle straight across to the west side of the island and make camp there.

Kayak friendly: Yes

Outfitters:
WILD ROCK OUTFITTERS
169 Charlotte Street
Peterborough, Ontario
K9J 2T7
705-745-9133

For more information:
TRENT-SEVERN WATERWAY
Box 567
Peterborough, Ontario
K9J 6Z6
705-742-9267

Topographical maps:
Burleigh Falls 31 D/9

Bon Echo Provincial Park

Okay, I'll admit it, there are moments when I really grow tired of cramming the bare essentials into a mildewed pack and heading off to explore some unknown canoe route. At times I just want to enjoy the familiar, to revisit a place I have gone back to year after year, just to relax in the simplicity of it all. That's why I love Bon Echo Provincial Park. It's a piece of accessible wilderness just 15 kilometers north of Cloyne, on the east side of Highway 41. The park offers not only sandy beaches and well-groomed campsites, but prime canoeing as well.

Paddlers have two main choices at the park. From the main campground, a leisurely daytrip — the Kishkebus canoe route — allows canoeists to explore the park's nature reserve zone on the east side of the Mazinaw Rock. And, for those who prefer to get away from the crowds of the main campground, there are twenty-five interior sites on Joeperry Lake that are only accessible by canoe.

My first pick is an overnight on Joeperry Lake. It's a relatively isolated place with plenty of prime campsites and a giant beach that extends all the way along the northeast shoreline. It does come with a price, however. To help keep it more remote, visitors must portage 600 meters down from the parking lot to reach the canoe launch site. Throughout the prime canoeing season, it's a good idea to phone ahead for reservations. The twenty-five sites offered (numbered from 501 to 525) can fill up quickly, and only the first half are situated on the more scenic portion of Joeperry Lake. Campsites 512 to 518 are in the southern half — a large wetland titled Pearson Lake — and when water levels are low, the sites can be extremely difficult to access. The main advantage to these sites is that the area provides excellent pike fishing right from shore.

A canoe cart can make life easier along the 600-meter portage into Bon Echo's Joeperry Lake.

Bon Echo's second option is a little less strenuous. For those canoeists who don't wish to give up the comforts offered at the main campground, especially the hot showers and flush toilets, you might want to reserve one of the 500 traditional sites on Mazinaw Lake and then head out for the day on the Kishkebus canoe route.

The park pamphlet that describes the 21-kilometer loop suggests that you head out in a clockwise direction. After having paddled this six-hour trip at least half a dozen times, I strongly disagree with the pamphlet. First, by traveling clockwise, you would most likely be forced to paddle against the prevailing winds while on Mazinaw Lake, the largest lake en route. And second, your first portage of the day would be the longest — a 1,500-meter trail between Mazinaw and Kishkebus Lake. If you head out counterclockwise, though, you have a good chance of having the wind help you instead of hinder you while out on Mazinaw. Also, if you have

A prime campsite, Joeperry Lake.

your longest portage of the day as your last, you may not feel up to it and simply decide to double back on your route rather than complete the circle.

You can begin the loop at a launch site provided near the main beach (unless you're lucky enough to reserve one of the six walk-in sites situated along the lakeshore). Also, directly across from the put-in, the park has provided a wooden dock and metal staircase that leads up to the top of Mazinaw Rock. Whether you choose to make the climb before or after your canoe trip, this 350-meter-high lookout is the focal point of Bon Echo and provides an exceptional way to view the surrounding landscape.

From the dock of the lookout trail, the canoe route follows the east shore of lower Mazinaw Lake until you reach the second bay. Here, at the far end of the bay, a quick lift-over to the right takes you into Campbell Creek.

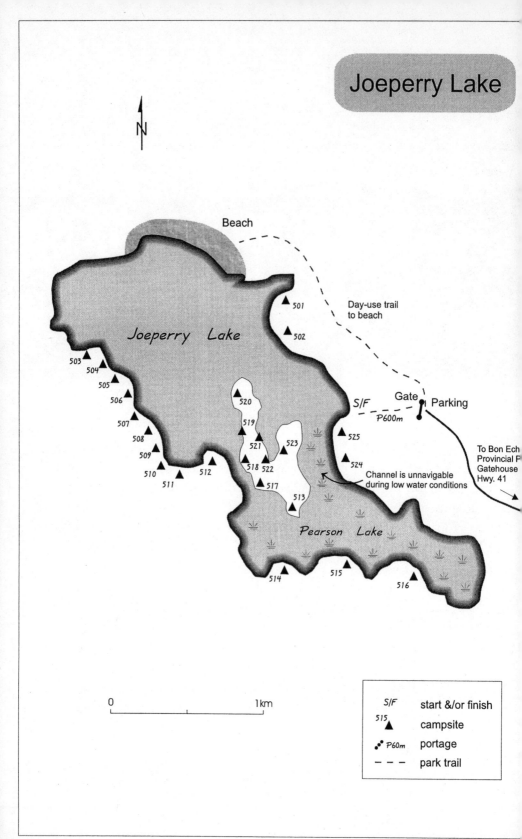

Joeperry Lake

N

Beach

Day-use trail
to beach

Joeperry Lake

▲ 501

▲ 502

503 ▲
504 ▲
505 ▲
506 ▲
507 ▲
508 ▲
509 ▲
510 ▲   ▲ 512
  511 ▲

▲ 520
519
▲ 521   ▲ 523
518 ▲ 522
  ▲ 517   513

S/F   Gate   Parking
P600m

▲ 525

▲ 524

Channel is unnavigable
during low water conditions

To Bon Ech
Provincial P
Gatehouse
Hwy. 41

▲

Pearson   Lake

▲ 514   ▲ 515   ▲ 516

0   1km

S/F	start &/or finish
515 ▲	campsite
P60m	portage
– – –	park trail

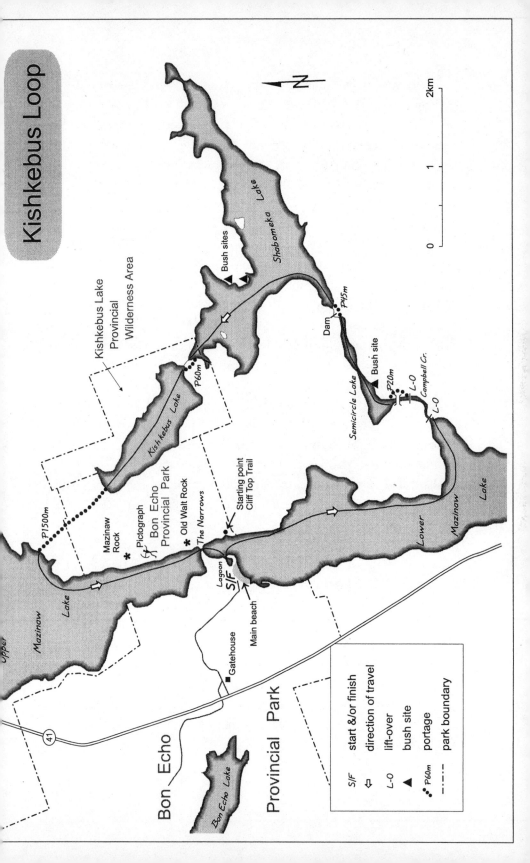

Another lift-over and a possible 20-meter portage to the right of an iron bridge, if water levels are low, soon follow. This takes you into Semicircle Lake (Horseshoe Lake), a scenic pond rumored to hold some good-size bass. By keeping to the right here and paddling upstream through a thick patch of pondweed, you'll eventually reach a second portage. It's a well-marked trail to the right of a concrete dam and is only 45 meters long.

You've now entered Shabomeka Lake (Shabomeka means "cranberry" in Ojibwa), or what's known locally as Buck Lake. Most of the shoreline here is privately owned and dotted with cottage lots. To the northeast, however, a couple of bush sites can be found along a strip of Crown land and can provide a suitable spot to stop for lunch.

I much prefer to push on to Kishkebus Lake before stopping for lunch. The portage, located at the far end of the Shabomeka's northwest bay, is an easy 60 meters marked to the left of a shallow creek.

Kishkebus is a part of the provincial park (no overnight camping is allowed) and an extension of the Mazinaw Cliff Nature Reserve. Totaling 743 hectares, the area protects a number of regionally significant species, including the rare prairie warbler and a large stand of the tolerant hardwoods that once dominated the area, before Kishkebus Lake housed an active logging camp in the early 1940s.

On the far side of Kishkebus, a small beach area marks the take-out for the 1,500-meter portage back to Mazinaw Lake. From here, you make the choice either to backtrack on your route or take on the all-encompassing but long and difficult portage. If you decide on the portage, it should take only thirty minutes to carry over to Mazinaw. It's a relatively flat trail, and you'll know you're close to the put-in when a cabin belonging to the Alpine Club of Canada appears on the left.

The reward for doing the long haul overland is a leisurely half-hour paddle alongside the impressive Mazinaw Rock, taking time out now and then to search for the 260 pictographs painted on slabs of granite just above the waterline — one of the largest concentrations of Native paintings in North America. It's a fantastic way to end such a fabulous trip.

Bon Echo Provincial Park

Difficulty:
Joeperry Lake is a perfect novice canoe route, but possible high winds on Mazinaw Lake and a lengthy portage make the Kishkebus loop a novice to intermediate route.

Portages:
Joe Perry Lake has one portage (a trail leading down from the parking lot to the canoe launch) and the Kishkebus loop has five portages.

Longest portage:
Joe Perry's longest is 500 meters and the longest for Kishkebus is 1,500 meters.

Fee:
A fee is required for overnight camping for both the main campground and Joe Perry Lake.

Alternative access: None

Alternative route:
To avoid the 1,500-meter portage on the Kishkebus loop, canoeists can backtrack once they reach Kishkebus Lake.

Kayak friendly:
Joeperry Lake is more suitable for kayakers than the Kishkebus loop because of the route's lengthy 1,500-meter portage.

Outfitters:
The main campground has a canoe rental service.

For more information:
BON ECHO PROVINCIAL PARK
R.R. 1
Cloyne, Ontario
K0H 1K0
613-336-2228

Maps:
The park has produced a pamphlet for both Joe Perry Lake and the Kishkebus loop.

Topographical maps:
Mazinaw 31 C/14

Crotch Lake has no portages — anywhere!

Crotch Lake

Crotch Lake (a rather inelegant name for such a beautiful place) is my favorite weekend getaway in eastern Ontario. I first camped here in 1994 while paddling the Mississippi River, and found it the most scenic spot en route. The lake's rocky shoreline, made up of what geologists call "muddy granite" (a whitish rock colored by calcium feldspar), provides excellent tent sites, and the only major development on the entire lake is Tumblehome Lodge, situated at the far southern end.

A public launch site is available for canoeists at the south end of the lake. You must first purchase a permit at Tumblehome Lodge, however. Originally there was no fee for camping on Crotch Lake, but because of heavy use, the municipality now charges for using the boat launch and a portion of the funds collected is used to maintain the assortment of campsites scattered along the Crown land shoreline.

To reach the lodge and then the boat launch, turn off Highway 7 and onto Highway 509. Head north for 9.6 kilometers and turn left onto Ardoch Road. The turnoff for the lodge is another 8.2 kilometers, on the right. Then, once you've got your permit, drive back out to Ardoch Road and head right. The access road is exactly 2 kilometers west and marked on the right-hand side. It is also possible to access the north end of the lake by way of an extremely rough road near the town of Ompah, but lately the road has been getting a little too bumpy for my liking.

Crotch Lake, named for being shaped like the crotch of a tree and not for any anatomical reason (though the crossroads of the nearby Ardock Road has been oddly named Bellybutton Centre), is divided into an upper and lower section that is joined by a narrow channel. To begin your paddle, simply head out of the southern bay

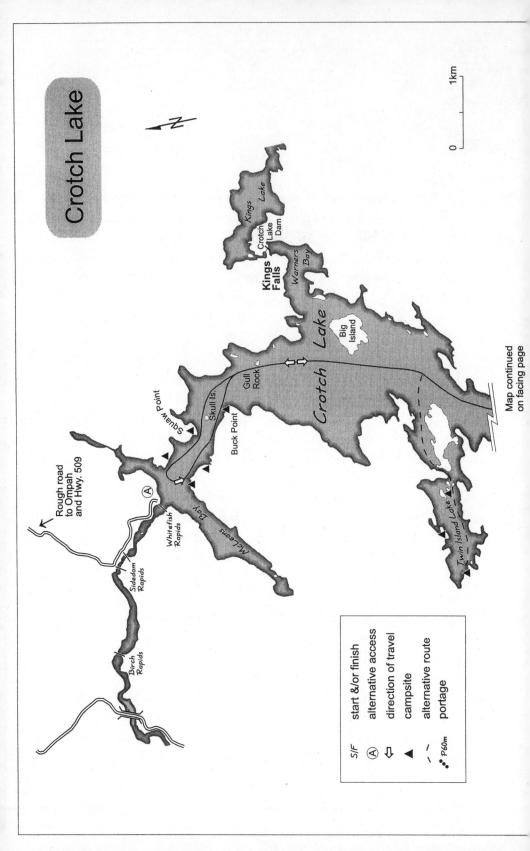

Crotch Lake

Kings Lake

Kings
Lake

Crotch
Lake
Dam

Kings
Falls

Warners Bay

Menbs Point

Skull Is.

Gull Rock

Big
Island

Buck Point

Crotch Lake

Rough road
to Ompah
and Hwy. 509

Ⓐ

Whitefish
Rapids

McLeans
Bay

Sidedam Rapids

Birch Rapids

Twin Island Lake

Map continued
on facing page

N

0   1km

S/F	start &/or finish
Ⓐ	alternative access
⇩	direction of travel
▲	campsite
– –	alternative route
•••• P60m	portage

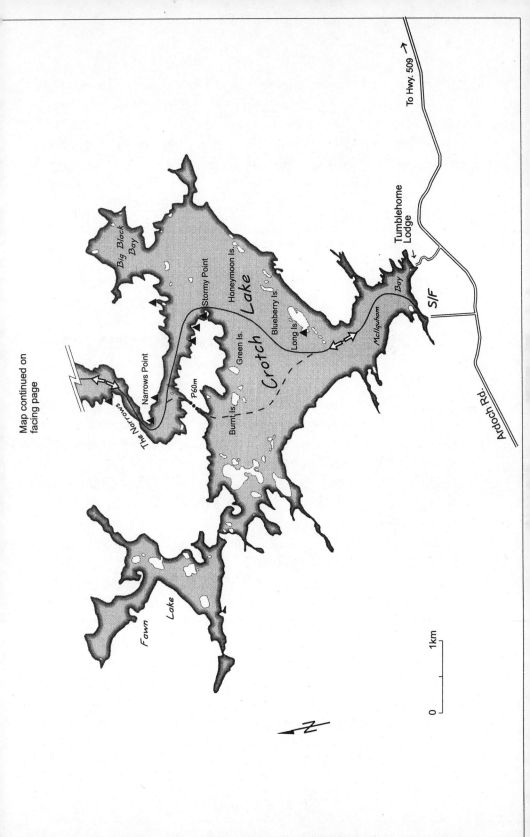

Map continued on
facing page

Big Black
Bay

The Narrows

Narrows Point

Stormy Point

Honeymoon Is.

Crotch Lake

Green Is.

Burnt Is.

P 60m

Blueberry Is.

Long Is.

McIlquham
Bay

Fawn Lake

Tumblehome
Lodge

S/F

To Hwy. 509 →

Ardoch Rd.

N

0   1km

where the boat launch is located (low water conditions may make this more difficult than usual). From here, head directly northwest toward Stormy Point and, after rounding the bend, stay to your left and follow the channel that eventually leads out into the north arm. Take note, however, that during high winds, Stormy Point can quickly become very dangerous. To avoid the exposed area, it is possible to make use of an unmarked portage located in a small bay to the north. The shortcut measures only 60 meters, but because of a buildup of driftwood tangled up in the bay, it may be difficult to reach the proper take-out.

Of course, it's not mandatory that you paddle all the way to the north arm. On my last trip to Crotch Lake, my wife and I ended up taking it extremely easy and we chose the first site we came to — a rocky cove equipped with a prime beach area. We would never have planned to stay here ourselves. (Alana and I had become so accustomed longer days on the water, much longer than a mere twenty minutes.) But we had invited a workmate, Darlene Craig, her son Ryan, her fiancé, Trevor McIlmoyle, and Ryan's friend Jason. It would be their first canoe trip, and our intention was to show the novice paddlers a few tricks of the trade.

In retrospect, however, the outing ended up having a unique twist to it. As usual, my wife and I packed along the same dehydrated meals and lightweight camping gear for the simple weekend excursion. On the other hand, Darlene's gang, knowing little about wilderness tripping, simply packed the essentials they regularly take with them car camping. Their canoes were loaded to the gunwales with two coolers full of juicy sirloins and an assortment of fresh vegetables. The young boys had equipped themselves with an unlimited supply of marshmallows, potato chips, soda pop, popcorn and roasted peanuts. Even a number of soft air mattresses, pillows to match, and ornamental lawn chairs found room somewhere in the bottom of their canoes.

Alana and I found ourselves smirking at all the gear the rest of the group had packed, at least until we all arrived at camp and were offered a share in a few of the luxuries they had brought along. To put it simply, the Crotch Lake route has no portages — anywhere. You just push off from the access point, paddle for as long as you wish, and then make camp. And for such an easy trip, who in their right mind wouldn't take a few comforts from home?

Needless to say, Darlene's group is planning our next trip together, and this time they are willing to show Alana and me few tricks of their own.

Crotch Lake

Time: 2 days

Difficulty: Novice

Portages: None

Fee:
A permit must be purchased at Tumblehome Lodge before using the government boat launch.

Alternative access:
The north end of the lake can be accessed by way of an extremely rough road near the town of Ompah.

Alternative route:
Twin Island Lake can be easily reached by a shallow channel on the southwest bay of Crotch Lake's North Arm.

Kayak friendly: Yes

Outfitters: None

For more information:
MINISTRY OF NATURAL RESOURCES
23 Spring Street
Box 70
Tweed, Ontario
K0K 3J0
613-478-2330

MISSISSIPPI VALLEY CONSERVATION AUTHORITY
Box 268
Lanark, Ontario
K0G 1K0
613-259-2421

TUMBLEHOME LODGE
Clarendon, Ontario
K0H 1J0
613-279-2414

Topographical maps:
Sharbot Lake 31 C/15

Depot Lakes Conservation Area

I'm guessing that few canoeists know about Depot Lakes Conservation Area. For years this out-of-the-way site had only a small campground on the second of its three lakes, and it wasn't until 1997 that a number of interior sites were added to help generate extra revenue for the park. Even though remote sites are now available, the area remains relatively unknown. I find this quite surprising. I've never seen such a place so perfect for a weekend of easy canoe camping. The main campground remains close by for use of the public beach and picnic facilities, the two additional lakes offer a place to head off for a day of exploring and exceptional fishing, and the use of motorboats is discouraged throughout the conservation area. In fact, the park has recently even banned those pesky Sea-Doos from the lake, which is a reason enough to give this unsung route a try.

To reach the park, head west off Highway 38 on to Snider Road. Follow the side road for 7 kilometers and then turn left at the T-intersection. The gatehouse is another 1.3 kilometers on your right, just past the Depot Creek bridge.

The Napanee Conservation Authority has managed the area since 1952, but it was the previous owners — the Rathbun Lumber Company — who gave the "depot lakes" their name. Camping depots for the logging company were established here when the land was cleared between the late 1800s and early 1900s. The area offered not only prime lumber (mostly maple and oak) but also a number of ways to transport it out to market. The Canadian Pacific Railway and a

Facing page: "Who says fishing is just for boys?" (Marin Hudson, Second Depot Lake).

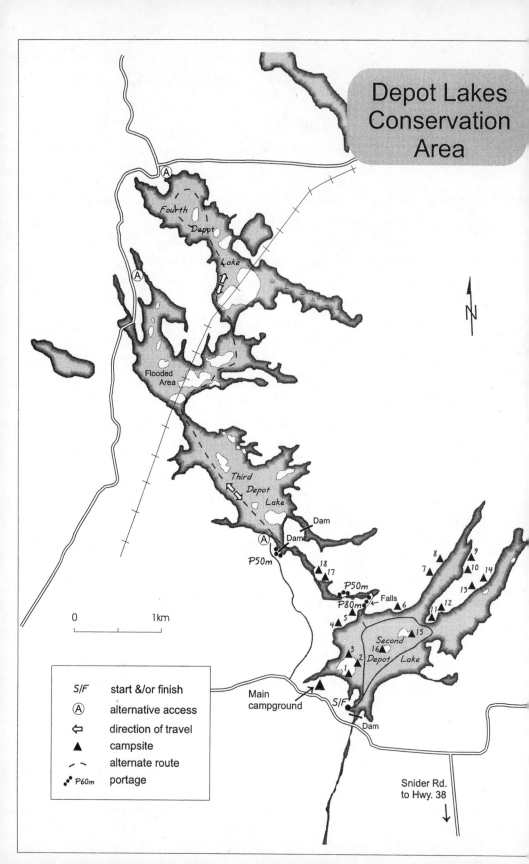

Depot Lakes Conservation Area

Fourth
Deppt
Lake

Flooded
Area

Third
Depot
Lake

Dam

Dam

P50m

18
17

P50m
P80m ← Falls

8   9
7   10   14
                13
     11 12
  6
4 5

15
16   Second
3   Depot   Lake
2
1

Main
campground

S/F

Dam

N

0   1km

S/F   start &/or finish

Ⓐ   alternative access

⇐   direction of travel

▲   campsite

- - -   alternate route

••• P60m   portage

Snider Rd.
to Hwy. 38
↓

series of colonization roads were built directly through the area and Depot Creek was even used to drive logs right up until 1908.

The logged-over areas have now been succeeded by second-growth forest. More impressive than the thick stands of trees, however, is the hard granite that they grow on. Known to geologists as the "rock knob upland," the sharp ridges that surround all three of the Depot Lakes were formed thousands of years ago when the Wisconsin Ice Field (the last glacier to have gone through this area) receded and left huge depressions that eventually filled with water. In ways both obvious and subtle, geological events such as this have given the park its special flavor. And the best way to appreciate this natural phenomenon is, of course, by canoe.

The main lake (Second Depot Lake) offers enough bays and inlets to explore for an entire day. But a much better option is to explore the Third and Fourth Depot Lakes to the north. You have two options to access the lakes. Either paddle back to the main campground and drive to one of the two launch sites provided, or take a series of short portages that connect Second Depot Lake with Third Depot Lake. I prefer the portages. Not only are they less bothersome than loading and unloading your canoe from the vehicle, the portages also offer a way to explore a section of Depot Creek that's home to a wide assortment of wildlife that includes turtles, muskrat, beaver, osprey and great blue herons.

To begin the portages, paddle to the northwest corner of Second Depot Lake. The first portage (80 meters) is marked to the left of where Depot Creek enters the lake. A quick paddle to the left leads you to the second portage (50 meters). It's marked on the right bank and avoids a section of fast water under an old iron bridge. The third and final portage (50 meters) is further along the marshy creek and marked on the far left side of the conservation authority dam. The trail, leading up the embankment to the parking area and public launch for Third Depot Lake, is the steepest en route, causing some canoeists to make use of a longer but somewhat easier trail leading up to Third Depot Lake on the right of the concrete dam.

Island campsite on Second Depot Lake, Depot Lakes Conservation Area.

Where to go once you've reached Third Depot Lake depends a lot on water levels. In high water conditions, you can easily reach Fourth Depot Lake by way of a narrow channel located under the railway line at the far northeast bay. There is a large flooded area northeast of the railway that can also be explored. In low water, however, you might be restricted to paddling around Third Depot Lake. Don't be too disappointed with the last choice, however. Third Depot Lake happens to be the most scenic of all three Depot Lakes. It also provides an excellent chance to catch a walleye, bass or a northern pike. Even if the fish aren't biting, a number of rock outcrops offer some great stopping places to enjoy your lunch and a refreshing swim before heading back to camp.

Depot Lakes Conservation Area

Time: 2 days

Difficulty: Novice

Portages:
3 (only necessary if you wish to explore neighboring lakes)

Longest portage: 80 meters

Fee:
An overnight camping fee is required (reservations are recommended).

Alternative access:
Third and Fourth Depot Lakes have their own separate launch site.

Alternative route:
Third and Fourth Depot Lakes offer a good day outing for canoeists.

Kayak friendly: Yes

Outfitters:
The main campground offers canoe rentals.

For more information:
QUINTE CONSERVATION
Main Office
Box 698, Belleville, Ontario
K8N 5B3
613-968-3434

DEPOT LAKES CONSERVATION
AREA / NAPANEE REGION
CONSERVATION AUTHORITY
25 Ontario Street West
Napanee, Ontario
K7R 3S6
613-354-3312
613-374-2940

Maps:
The Napanee Region Conservation Authority has produced a pamphlet, *Depot Lakes Conservation Area.*

Topographic Maps:
Tichborne 31 C/10

Murphys Point Provincial Park

Murphys Point Provincial Park, situated along the Rideau Waterway, is one of those typical campgrounds that, at times, can become a little overwhelmed with nosey neighbors and yappy dogs. However, the area — a natural landscape of mineral-rich Canadian Shield bedrock surrounded by gentle farmland, enlivened by a good number of small-town flea markets and antiques stores — has always intrigued me and my wife. So when we heard that a new system of canoe-in campsites was being added to the park, we jumped at the chance and phoned ahead for reservations.

The provincial park is located off Highway 21, 19 kilometers south of Perth at the top of Big Rideau Lake. Less than a kilometer from the park entrance, the road forks, with the park store and canoe rentals on the right and the main gatehouse on the left.

After picking up our permit at the gatehouse we drove down to the designated launch site on the far east side of the park. (A second launch site can be used at the administration dock in Noble Bay.) From here we paddled straight out to Big Rideau Lake (be careful not to mistake the entrance to Hoggs Bay, to your immediate right, for Rideau Lake) and headed south for a mere half kilometer before pulling up on the first of four cluster sites situated throughout the park. Of the four boat-in sites, this is the only site that remains exclusively for use by canoeists. Then, after being serenaded by a family of loons gathering just off our campsite and entertained by a beaver attempting to steal some of our precious firewood for the construction of its nearby lodge, we dozed off beside a cozy fire and eventually drifted off to bed. For once, it was nice to stay at a busy

Facing page: Bailey and Alana stop for coffee along the portage (Murphy's Point Provincial Park).

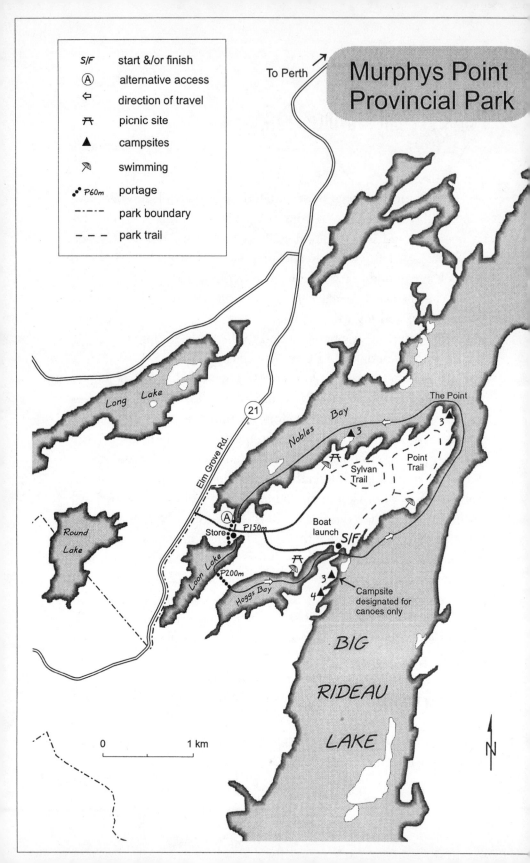

The Point, Big Rideau Lake.

provincial park, making use of all the amenities but also free of such problems as drunken campers staggering past our tent or bothersome raccoons scratching at the truck of our car in search of improperly stored edibles.

Early the next morning we packed a picnic and headed off on the park's 8-kilometer canoe loop. The route only takes about two and a half hours to complete, but we planned to have brunch halfway along, stop for a swim at the public beach, and even portage to the park store for a coffee and fresh pastry. It was a luxurious canoe trip, to say the least.

The route can be traveled in both directions. Alana and I, however, wanting to beat the high winds as well as the heavy boat traffic out on Big Rideau Lake, decided on paddling the big water first. Heading counterclockwise we went north, had our picnic on what's known as "The Point" — a big knob of granite at the far northeast end of the park — and then headed to the nearby beach to indulge in the cool sky-blue waters of the Big Rideau.

By midday we had made our way to the far end of Nobles Bay. We then took the 150-meter portage to the park store (and café) and eventually to the north shore of Loon Lake. Here, another 200-meter trail was marked to the southeast corner of the lake, taking us to Hoggs Bay, where we slowly made our way back to Big Rideau Lake and our base camp, to once again listen to the cry of the loons and defend our woodpile from the neighboring beaver.

Murphys Point Provincial Park

Time: 1 to 2 days

Difficulty: Novice

Portages: 2

Longest portage: 200 meters

Fee:
An overnight camping permit must be purchased.

Alternative access:
The Noble Bay boat launch, located just to the left of the main gatehouse, can also be used as an access point.

Alternative route: No

Kayak friendly: Yes

Outfitters:
Canoes can be rented from the park store.

For more information:
MURPHYS POINT
PROVINCIAL PARK
R.R. 5
Perth, Ontario
K7H 3C7
613-267-5060
For reservations call
1-888-668-7275

Topographical maps:
Perth 31 C/16

Charleston Lake Provincial Park

Many canoeists associate true wilderness paddling with the Canadian Shield — a great slab of ancient rock more obvious in northern parks such as Algonquin or Quetico. To the east, however, this two-billion-year-old rock also dominates the landscape by way of a southern extension known as the Frontanac Axis. And because of this, Charleston Lake Provincial Park is also added to the list of the province's prime canoe destinations.

The rugged, northern character of the Charleston Lake area has always been best suited for the pursuits of outdoor enthusiasts, as settlers found the thin soils unproductive. As far back as the 1860s, the lake itself had become a well-known retreat for upper-class vacationers from Ottawa, Toronto and Upper New York State who found pleasure in exploring the lake by steamer, fancy sailboats, or cedar-strip guide boats rowed by a single oarsman.

Present-day canoeists now seem to dominate the recreational scene by making use of a number of lakes, rivers and creeks in the area. (Charleston Lake – Red Horse Lake – Gananoque River and Wilts Creek is the most popular weekend loop.) However, the provincial park, situated on the southwest corner of Charleston Lake, does offer the best canoeing overall, especially when low water levels can make the extended routes unnavigable throughout most of the paddling season.

The park itself was created after Professor A. J. E. Child, a strong member of the Federation of Ontario Naturalists, offered to sell his land for the development of a provincial wilderness recreation area in 1962. Two years later, Professor Child's 5-kilometer shoreline, between Slacks Bay and Runnings Bay, and later, a total of 2,334 hectares of land (including eleven Crown land islands), were protected for their biological, cultural and aesthetic features.

The rugged scenery of Charleston Lake has enticed outdoor enthusiasts to the area as far back as the 1860s.

Charleston Lake Provincial Park is located northeast of Kingston and can be reached by County Road 3 from Highway 42 and Highway 15 and the Lansdowne turnoff from Highway 401.

The main campground maintains 238 sites but the park also offers 13 interior sites organized into clusters grouped together at Bob's Cove, Hidden Cove, Buckhorn Bay, Captain Gap, Slim Bay and Covey's Gap. Each cluster has one to three campsites and can hold six people and three tents per site. There is a canoe launch and parking lot at the far end of the main campground, past the interpretive center and second beach.

It's wise to reserve well in advance for the more remote sites, especially the cluster site located in Slim Bay, where powerboats have been banned because the area is the only known nesting site for loons in the park. (The southern portion of Runnings Bay is also off-limits to powerboats.)

Conveniently connected to each interior site is a hiking trail upon which visitors can head off to explore the area's wide assortment of flora and fauna. Since the Frontenac Axis is the most southern part of the Shield, the various habitats that are found here create what biologists call a transition zone. Here, a large selection of plants and animals occur either beyond the normal southern or northern extent of their range, and Charleston Lake has some of the rarest finds in the province. Rooted along a narrow valley in Tallow Rock Bay, as well as a southern portion of Slim Bay, is a collection of showy orchis growing at the base of mature hemlock. Pitch pine, which was once used to seal wooden boats and is one of Canada's scarcest tree species, is also found in good concentration on the quartzite ridge north of Duck Bay. And Charleston Lake's unofficial mascot is the black rat snake — a harmless 2-meter-long tree-climbing constrictor that, when startled, will flatten out its neck and vibrate its tail.

This area is so rich in wildlife, it's no wonder that the Native tribes used it extensively for more than 3,000 years, mostly as a seasonal stopover for small nomadic hunting bands. The neighboring

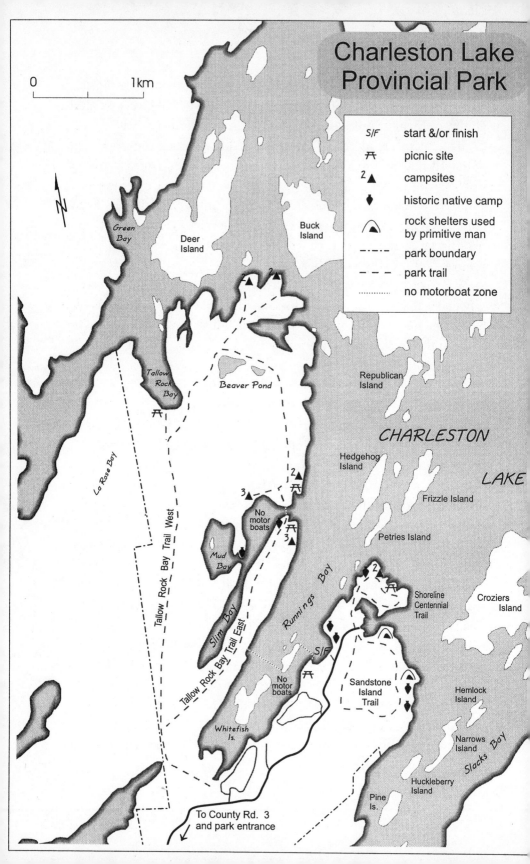

Alana makes note of the no motorboat policy in Charleston Lake's Slim Bay.

lakes, especially Red Horse Lake, contain significant evidence of Native use. But Charleston Lake is the most popular spot for archaeological investigations. More than twenty small prehistoric campsites have been located in and along the numerous bays and peninsulas.

Three main archaeological sites that you can easily visit by canoe include the pictographs in Slim Bay and the mysterious rock shelters found at Jackson's Point and Gordon Rock. The rock paintings have become harder to spot over the years, but the rock shelters, thought to be used by primitive man, are quite noticeable to canoeists cruising the shoreline. The caves were formed when weaker layers of quartzite pebbles crumbled beneath the more resistant sandstone.

These biological and cultural treasures abound in Charleston Lake, but it's still the scenic appeal of the rugged landscape, much like the land more to the north, that has influenced both the natural and human history of the area and that will continue to draw canoeists to this semi-wilderness area of eastern Ontario. Believe me, it's worth a visit!

Charleston Lake Provincial Park

Difficulty: Novice

Portages: None

Fee:
A fee is required for overnight camping.

Alternative access: None

Alternative route:
You can plan a circle route by canoeing Charleston Lake – Red Horse Lake – Gananoque River and Wilts Creek. (Ask the park staff for information.)

Kayak friendly: Yes

Outfitters:
The main campground offers canoe rentals.

For more information:
CHARLESTON LAKE
PROVINCIAL PARK
148 Woodvale Road
Lansdowne, Ontario
K0E 1L0
613-659-2065

Maps:
Charleston Lake Provincial Park has produced a map, *Charleston Provincial Park.*

Topographical maps:
Westport 31 C/9

Grants Creek / Pooh Lake

It doesn't seem to matter how busy work gets, I always manage to make it down to the coffee room at least once a day. Not for the coffee, of course. The stuff tastes like shoe leather. It's the conversations with my fellow workmates that draw me down to the basement. You see, there's a group of us who have promised never to talk about anything except canoeing while taking in our daily caffeine fix.

One instructor, Hugh Banks, takes this pledge very seriously. Whenever someone mentions a problem with his students or makes some political statement about the college administration, he changes the subject by quickly blurting out, "So where's our next canoe trip, Kevin?" To help his scheme, I simply fire back the name of some obscure place that no one has ever heard about, and the conversation is quickly turned back toward the desired subject — canoeing.

A number of great adventures have been formed this way. Of course, the best one to date was when I mentioned a possible trip to Pooh Lake — named by a former Algonquin Park ranger after author A. A. Milne's 1926 story, *Winnie the Pooh*. That definitely got everyone's attention. I remember it took three cups of coffee to explain all the details to a very fixed audience.

There are two ways to reach Pooh Lake, located just outside of Algonquin Provincial Park's eastern boundary. The first is to paddle up Grants Creek — a new and unmaintained Waterway Park developed through the Lands for Life (Ontario's Living Legacy) project of 1999. And the second is a bumpy ride down the Menet Lake Road, marked on the left side of Highway 17, just north of Driftwood Provincial Park and a few kilometers south of where Grants Creek flows into the Ottawa River.

If you happen to be in a hurry to reach Pooh Lake, and your vehicle can manage the rough ride, then the Menet Lake Road is

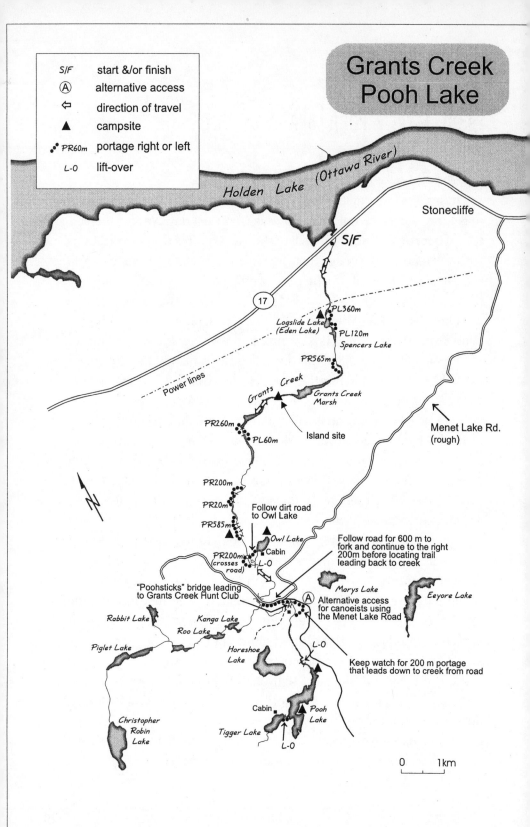

Grants Creek
Pooh Lake

S/F	start &/or finish
Ⓐ	alternative access
⇐	direction of travel
▲	campsite
•••• PR60m	portage right or left
L-O	lift-over

Holden Lake (Ottawa River)

Stonecliffe

S/F

17

Logslide Lake (Eden Lake)

PL360m

PL120m

Spencers Lake

PR565m

Power lines

Grants Creek

Grants Creek Marsh

Island site

Menet Lake Rd. (rough)

PR260m

PL60m

PR200m

PR20m

Follow dirt road to Owl Lake

PR585m

Owl Lake

Cabin

PR200m (crosses road)

L-O

Follow road for 600 m to fork and continue to the right 200m before locating trail leading back to creek

"Poohsticks" bridge leading to Grants Creek Hunt Club

Ⓐ Alternative access for canoeists using the Menet Lake Road

Marys Lake

Eeyore Lake

Rabbit Lake

Kanga Lake

Roo Lake

Piglet Lake

Horeshoe Lake

L-O

Keep watch for 200 m portage that leads down to creek from road

Christopher Robin Lake

Cabin

Tigger Lake

Pooh Lake

L-O

N

0   1km

your best bet. Simply follow the main dirt road for approximately 10 kilometers, and then take the side road to the left just before the main road crosses Grants Creek. A short portage is marked on the right side of the roadway, just past where a bridge crosses over the creek to a cabin owned by the Grants Creek Hunt Club. It's another twenty-minute paddle upstream from here to Pooh Lake, with a few exposed rocks and a large beaver dam to lift over just before you get to the lake.

Hugh and I decided to paddle the entire stretch of Grants Creek, however. We were accompanied by Hugh's ten-year-old son, Jeremy, and we thought the unmaintained route up Grants Creek would introduce the youngster to the realities of canoe tripping. Besides, the cold-water stream looked awfully promising for brook trout fishing.

Well, we were wrong about the fishing. None of us caught a single trout. But the trip up, and eventually back down, Grants Creek happened to be Jeremy's first real adventure in a canoe.

The escapades began almost immediately. The government sign that marks the parking area north of the Grants Creek bridge and on the left side of Highway 17 was hidden by brush, and we ended up parking south of the bridge and wading up a series of rapids before realizing our mistake. Then, after a long, 2-kilometer section of river blocked by three consecutive beaver dams, we endured the first of the route's ten rough and incredibly steep portages. The first portage is marked to the left and climbs alongside a scenic cascade for a short 360 meters.

After a quick paddle across Logslide Lake (once used to hold logs before being flushed down into the Ottawa River come spring), the second portage is marked to the left of yet another waterfall. The path measures only 120 meters but it heads directly up a slab of granite and happens to be the steepest portage en route.

Soon a third portage, to the right, is marked at the end of Spencers Lake. It's not as abrupt as the first two, but it's difficult to locate at times and measures a full 565 meters.

Hugh Banks, son Jeremy, and our mascot — a stuffed Winnie the Pooh bear — lead the way up Grants Creek.

From here it's a leisurely hour's paddle across the expanse of Grants Creek Marsh, alive with various species of ducks, great blue herons, muskrat and beaver. Throughout the expansive marsh a few outcrops of rock carpeted in white pine present themselves as places to pull up on shore for a lunch break. A prime campsite is even marked on a central island and can be a great place as long as the bug population stays down.

The next series of portages begins close to the far west end, where the creek empties into the marsh. There are two trails here. The first measures 260 meters and is marked on the right of a minor waterfall, and the second is only 60 meters and marked on the left of a large rock pile.

After a good kilometer of almost stagnant water, the shoreline grows rugged once again and another string of portages now avoid one of the most impressive drops along Grants Creek. The first portage is a straightforward 200-meter path leading around the right of a gigantic water slide. The next is a mere 20-meter carry to the right of a rock-strewn chute. But the third portage, also found to the right, is an extensive 585-meter, poorly maintained pathway squeezed through a miniature canyon. This is the most frustrating portage along the creek, both because the rough path is dangerously steep in places, not to mention blocked by a number of fallen trees, and because a series of side trails heading back down to the creek makes the main trail almost impossible to locate at times.

Disgruntled about accidentally exploring three of the five side trails, Hugh strongly suggested that we make camp halfway along the portage. It was a bush site (since the route is no longer maintained, the selection of designated campsites is an almost impossible task), but the cleared area came with a plot of soft moss to erect the tent on and a flat rock to use as a handy dinner table. In fact, it was such a perfect, out-of-the-way spot along the flooded creek that we decided to make it our base camp and make tomorrow's paddle up to Pooh Lake into an easy daytrip. This would rid us of dragging all our gear upstream through the unexplored route and reduce our trip from four days to an easy three.

So early the next morning, after hanging our food pack between two old pine trees, we loaded our canoe up with our lunch bags and fishing gear, and continued our upstream journey.

Another portage, a 200-meter trail marked to the right of an iron bridge, is quick to block the route again. The path crosses a dirt road about three-quarters the way along, and a five-minute walk across the bridge and up the road will take you on a side trip into Owl Lake. Keeping with the Winnie the Pooh theme, our group took time out to explore the oval-shaped pond. We even took a few casts from shore to try and catch at least one of the many good-sized brook trout that are rumored to hole up on the bottom of Owl Lake. However, an hour later, not even Jeremy, the best angler among us, had hooked a fish, and so we decided that we would continue on up the creek and spend our energy on the not-so-renowned rainbow trout stocked in Pooh Lake.

Except for a quick swift, followed by a large beaver dam, both of which have to be dragged over almost immediately after the last portage, the creek remains sluggish right up until the Menet Lake Road crossing.

Hugh, Jeremy and I were a little confused as to our whereabouts at this point. An old Algonquin map, dating back to 1971, was the only thing that we could find before heading out on our trip that had a description of the Grants Creek canoe route, and so far the map had proved only somewhat accurate. At this point, however, it became totally useless. The map showed a 200-meter portage and 345-meter portage on the left bank and no sign of any road crossing. We figured that splitting up was our best option, with Hugh and Jeremy walking the dirt road to the south and me paddling further up the creek.

An hour later, after finding no portages and having to slug over boulders and gnarled spruce trees fallen across the creek like matchsticks, I finally met Hugh and Jeremy sitting on top of a metal bridge, enjoying a game of "Pooh Sticks." (The game originated in

A. A. Milne's *The House at Pooh Corner* and involves dropping sticks into the stream and seeing which one appears on the other side of the bridge first.)

Obviously, the road is the better route. First, go left from the bridge and walk uphill for approximately 600 meters until you reach a fork in the road. Then go right to where you'll eventually see the old Pooh Stick bridge crossing over to the Grants Creek Hunt Camp. Here, remain on the main road on the left side of the creek and look to the right where a 200-meter path will lead you back down to the water.

From here it's only a 20-minute paddle through a large marsh, followed by another shallow swift and beaver dam that must be lifted over (we couldn't find another 300-meter portage that the old map had marked to the left), before you reach the very scenic Pooh Lake. (Christopher Robin, Piglet and Eeyore Lake are also nearby but far too difficult to reach by canoe.)

There is a campsite on a pine-clad point about halfway across Pooh Lake. Our group's plan, however, was to troll our fishing lines directly across the lake, then make a quick "bounce" into Tigger Lake (a short lift-over connects this small pond with Pooh Lake's northwest bay) for a well-deserved shore lunch of fried trout. But even with our trip's mascot — a stuffed Winnie the Pooh bear — tied onto the canoe's bowplate for good luck, we remained fishless and had to resort to stale honey sandwiches for our afternoon meal.

By midday we gave up any hope of catching fish (Jeremy figured they were taken by a gang of Heffalumps) and headed back to base camp. Along the way, rejoicing at finally being able to travel with the current, our spirits remained surprisingly high for three avid anglers returning with an empty stringer. After all, didn't Winnie the Pooh once say about his "Expodition" to the North Pole, "We might find something that we weren't looking for, which might be just what we were looking for, really."? To me, that's what canoe tripping on Grants Creek was all about.

Grants Creek / Pooh Lake

Time: 3 to 4 days

Difficulty:
Moderate canoe-tripping experience is needed if you wish to travel upstream on Grants Creek.

Portages: 11

Longest portage: 900 meters

Fee:
This is an unmaintained provincial park and no fee is required.

Alternative access:
You can avoid most of Grants Creek by using Menet Lake Road to access Pooh Lake.

Alternative route:
A side trip to Owl Lake can be had by following the dirt road that crosses the ninth portage en route.

Kayak friendly:
Grants Creek is not ideally suited for kayaks, but you can avoid the creek by directly accessing Pooh Lake by way of Menet Lake Road.

Outfitters:
VALLEY VENTURES
Box 1115
Deep River, Ontario
K0J 1P0
613-584-2577

For more information:
MINISTRY OF NATURAL RESOURCES
Pembroke District Office
31 Riverside Drive
Box 220
Pembroke, Ontario
K8A 6X4
613-732-3661

Topographical maps:
Rolphton 31 K/4
Brent 31 L/1

Before You Go

Sometimes I think organizing for a trip is more fun than the actual trip itself. First, there's finding the perfect route. The maps are rolled out across the kitchen floor, the websites are browsed through, and a whole assortment of guidebooks are purchased or checked out from the library. Then, when you finally decided on the destination, which is more often than not the same place you went to last year, you pass the time waiting for the weekend to come around by preparing the gear. The smoke-scented packs are brought down from the attic, blackened cookpots are given a quick wash, and the tent is unrolled in the backyard to check for any signs of mildew. Then there are meals to decide on and the difficult decision is made on whether to purchase the regular freeze-dried meals from the local outdoor store or to try your luck at making up your own recipes for a change.

To help make all these plans come together, I've decided to add two things this book: a checklist of camping gear and a few of my favorite recipes to try. The checklist is more of a "have I forgotten anything" list, and you should by no means consider it the ultimate inventory, meant for everyone. Also, the recipes I've included only represent a few of the possible alternative ways to prepare your own nutritious lightweight meals instead of buying that store-bought freeze-dried stuff, which, for some unknown reason, has a tendency to give me gas. You can use your own ingenuity to come up with your own list and recipes.

Have You Forgotten Anything?

Clothes (for a two-to-four-day trip)

- two cotton or canvas shirts
- two T-shirts
- one wool sweater or fleece top
- two extra pair of socks
- one extra pair of underwear
- two pairs of pants (no blue jeans)
- one pair of shorts (doubles as swimsuit if you're not into skinny dipping)
- hiking boots
- sneakers, moccasins or sport sandals for around camp
- bug hat (finer mesh for blackfly season)
- bandanna (useful for spraying bug dope on rather than directly onto your skin)
- hat
- rain gear (make sure to keep it handy, on the top of your pack)
- good sunglasses

Alana and Bailey prepare for the first of three portages leading into Noganosh.

Toiletries

- beach towel
- portable toothbrush and toothpaste (small travel sizes can usually be purchased at drugstore)
- toilet paper (store in resealable plastic bag)
- hairbrush
- biodegradable soap
- hairband
- razor
- contact lens solution
- extra pair of glasses
- birth control

Kitchen Set

- one medium and one small cooking pot with lids, and non-stick frying pan (to avoid expensive cooking sets, purchase all three separately at department store and simply remove handles)
- plastic travel mug
- metal plate (plastic frisbee can also be used as a plate, bowl and toy for the beach)
- hard plastic spoon and metal fork
- metal or plastic spatula
- aluminum foil
- campstove with extra fuel container and funnel
- waterproof matches in waterproof container, plus a butane lighter
- scouring pad and sponge mixture
- tea towel
- pair of utility gloves for grabbing cooking pot off the fire
- lightweight saw
- water bottle(s)
- water purification gadget (water filter)
- spices, jam, peanut butter, coffee, sugar, maple syrup, honey, margarine, in plastic containers
- meals packed in separate containers and in one large food bag (complete with instructions and clearly labeled).

Sleeping Gear

- tent
- ground sheet that fits inside tent
- large rain tarp
- sleeping bag
- Therm-a-rest or foam pad

Packs

- external or internal frame pack
- various stuff sacks for clothes and other items
- separate pack/barrel for food
- daypack
- camera bag

Items Required by Law to Have in Canoe

- two 30-meter lengths of nylon rope stuffed in a throwbag
- flashlight
- whistle
- approved and properly fitting PFD (personal flotation device)
- bailer
- extra paddle

Individual Items

- maps
- waterproof map case
- compass
- bug dope
- hand lotion
- sunscreen
- camera, film and
- extra batteries
- playing cards, cribbage board, etc.
- fishing license
- camping permit
- first-aid kit
- repair kit

"There's a blackfly in my Chardonnay."

- roll of duct tape
- extra resealable bags
- a couple of strong
  garbage bags
- journal and pencil
- paperback novel
- hammock

- bird, tree, animal-track
  identification guide
- binoculars
- star chart
- fishing rod and compact
  tackle box
- pocketknife

Food for Thought

Food has to be one of the more important items to pack for a canoe trip. A combination of protein, vegetables and starch has long been the staple diet needed for refueling the body while venturing out in the wilds, especially when you find yourself having to go beyond your usual physical and mental abilities while on that surprisingly long portage or against high winds out on a exposed lake.

Camp meals should be nourishing, lightweight, easy and quick to prepare, not to mention palatable. Dried foods sold in regular outdoor shops are ideal for canoeists, capturing a miniature lightweight and bacteria-free replica of home-style meals. But don't stop there. A number of other possible meals can be created by shopping at grocery or bulk-food stores. By combining seasoning packages with simple cooking staples (lentils, rice, pasta, soy grits, couscous, bulgur, quinoa, etc.) many canoeists have created some of the fanciest gourmet meals.

The ultimate test of choosing the best recipe is to invite your friends over for dinner before you go canoe camping. Then sit them down to a glass of wine and feed them camp dishes such as Mushroom Bulgur Bonanza, Mountain Gruel, or a spicy Moroccan Couscous. Make them believe, of course, that you have spent all day in the kitchen cooking up the gourmet meals, not twenty minutes over a campstove out on the back porch. If your guests enjoy the meal, pack the recipe up in a resealable bag for your next trip. If they feed it to the dog, then just go out and buy a box of Kraft Dinner until next the trip.

What follows are a few recipes that haven't failed me yet.

Facing page: Len Lockwood prepares the first layer of a triple-layer Black Forest cake.

Meatless Stroganoff

1 large package cream of mushroom soup mix

2 cups noodles (any style)

2 Tbs. dehydrated mushrooms

2 Tbs. dehydrated leek

1 cube beef bouillon

pinch of paprika

pinch of black pepper

pinch of garlic powder

2½ cups water

Add bouillon cube to water and bring to a boil. Add rest of ingredients except for paprika, black pepper and garlic, and let simmer until noodles are cooked and vegetables are rehydrated. Pour out excess water and add spices to desired flavor.

Moroccan Couscous

1 cup couscous

1½ tsp. curry powder

1 cube vegetable bouillon

¼ cup dehydrated red and green peppers

4–5 diced sundried tomatoes

¼ cup pistachios

1 clove of garlic

1½ cups water

Bring water to a boil and mix in all ingredients. Over a moderate heat, cook 1 to 2 minutes. Let sit off heat for 3 more minutes.

Mexican-style Couscous

2½ cups water

1 cup couscous

1 cube vegetable bouillon

2 Tbs. dried vegetables

2 Tbs. dried red and green
peppers

2 Tbs. dried corn

¼ cup mixture of black
beans and red organic
beans

1 tsp. onion powder

1 tsp. parsley

1 clove of garlic

1 can of dehydrated tomato
paste

Pre-soak the beans in a container
(a spare Nalgene bottle works well)
for an entire day. Then, to prepare the
dish, first reconstitute tomato paste in
½ cup of boiling water with the dried
vegetables, dried peppers and dried
corn. Set the sauce aside and boil
beans in 1 cup of water for 20
minutes. Then, place the cooked
beans in with the couscous — mixed
with the vegetable bouillon, onion
powder, parsley and garlic — and let
boil in 1 cup of water for 1 to 2
minutes. Finally, add the tomato
sauce and serve.

Quinoa Curry

1 cup quinoa (grain from
Peru)

1 fresh red onion

½ teaspoon salt

2 teaspoons curry powder

handful of dried pears,
dates, apricots, chopped
almonds

Bring three cups of water to a boil
and add quinoa mixture. Grain is
ready when it looks transparent. Let
stand covered for 10 minutes.

Mock Shepherd's Pie

1 cup pre-cooked rice

1 cup breadcrumbs

1 cup mixed dehydrated
vegetables (peas,
carrots, onion, green
pepper)

¼ cup dehydrated
mushrooms

pinch of parsley

pinch of garlic powder

½ cup of bulgar

1 cup potato flakes

1 cube beef bouillon

dash of Worcestershire
sauce

1 tsp. tomato or spaghetti
sauce powder

Combine the pre-cooked rice, vegetables, mushrooms, parsley, garlic powder, beef bouillon cube, and tomato powder into 2 cups boiling water and let simmer for 5 minutes. Remove from heat and mix in breadcrumbs. Let stand for 5 minutes. Then place bulgar into 2 cups boiling water and let simmer for 5 minutes. Add a dash of Worcestershire sauce and combine with the rice and breadcrumbs. Finally, slowly add water to potato flakes until fluffy and place on top.

Shrimp Alfredo

1 dehydrated package of
Alfredo sauce

1 can of dehydrated small
shrimp

2 cups noodles (any style)

¼ cup dried veggies

1 Tbs Parmesan

Add noodles, shrimp and veggies to 2 cups boiling water and simmer for 12 minutes. Reconstitute dehydrated Alfredo sauce in ½ cup boiling water and stir into noodles. Top with Parmesan cheese.

That's Italian

2 cups noodles (any style)

1 13-oz. can of dehydrated
tomato paste

1 Tbs. dried spaghetti sauce

¼ cup mixture of dehydra-
ted eggplant, red and green
peppers, onion, black
olives and mushrooms

¼ cup Parmesan cheese

4½ cups water

Reconstitute tomato paste in ½ cup of boiling water with dried spaghetti sauce. Add noodles, vegetables and mushrooms to 4 cups boiling water and let simmer until noodles are cooked. Pour out excess water and add tomato paste. Sprinkle cheese on top.

Sweet and Sour Rice Dish

2 cups water

½ cup rice (brown is good)

1 cup mixture of dried fruit
(pineapple, apricot,
apples and raisins)

¼ cup mixture of walnuts
and almonds

dash of garlic

dash of black pepper

2 Tbs. brown sugar

1½ Tbs. soy sauce (save a
packet from your take-out
order of Chinese food)

1½ Tbs. vinegar (pocket a packet
from your local burger joint)

1 Tbs. cooking oil

Place rice and fruit mixture into 2 cups boiling water and let simmer until rice is done (brown rice takes about 20 minutes). Drain excess water. Add nuts, sugar, spices, soy sauce and vinegar and then fry in oil for 5 to 7 minutes. For variety, add a can of chicken or dehydrated chicken or pork.

Moroccan couscous stuffed in a pita is my all-time favorite lunchtime snack.

Easy Pasta Parmesan

2 cups noodles (any style)

4 cups water

2 Tbs. margarine

2 Tbs. dried vegetables (green pepper, red pepper, carrots, onion flakes, etc.)

2 Tbs. dried mushrooms

4 sun dried tomatoes, chopped

1 tsp. red wine (optional)

1 package pasta parmesan noodle sauce

handful of shelled pistachio nuts

(grated cheese optional)

Bring water to a boil in a pot. Add noodles, dried vegetables, mushrooms, pistachio nuts and tomatoes. Let simmer until noodles are cooked and vegetables have rehydrated. Pour out excess water and add margarine, red wine and noodle sauce, stirring until well mixed and the margarine is melted. Serve with grated cheese.

Pita Pizza

2 pita breads (more if needed)

1 can of dehydrated tomato paste (paste to be dehydrated at home, or use dried spaghetti sauce)

2 Tbs. green and red pepper

1 fresh onion (any kind)

1 dried salami (or other dried meats)

grated cheese (any kind)

1 Tbs. olive oil

Coat pan with olive oil. Prepare toppings on pizza. Place pizza in pan and cover for 5 to 7 minutes on a cookstove (longer over the fire). Cut up into pieces and share while the next pizza is being prepared and cooked.

🔥 Toppings can be changed to suit personalities; just remember to keep it light and stick to food not easily spoiled.

Strawberry Turnovers

1 cup dehydrated
strawberries

1 cup Tea-Bisk or
Bisquick mix

flour for kneading

2 Tbs. of cognac

3 Tbs. brown sugar

1 Tbs. olive oil

¾ cup water

Let strawberries reconstitute in ½ cup of water, cognac and brown sugar. Mix Tea-Bisk or Bisquick with ¼ cup water. Knead handful portions in flour, spread flat and place in oiled deep-dish frying pan or shallow cooking pot. Add a glob of strawberries to one side of dough and flip opposite side over top. Press down on corners, cover pan and let bake at a low temperature for 7 to 8 minutes.

Simple Cinnamon Rolls

3 cups Tea-Bisk or
Bisquick mix

½ cup brown sugar

1 Tbs. cinnamon

¼ cup raisins

3 Tbs. margarine

flour for rolling

1 Tbs. olive oil

¼ cup water

Slowly add water to Tea-Bisk or Bisquick to from dough and roll out on floured canoe paddle. Spread margarine onto flattened surface (a paddle works well), sprinkling cinnamon, brown sugar and raisins. Roll into a log and slice 1-inch slices and place them in oiled frying pan. Cover and bake over low heat for 7 to 8 minutes.

Tortilla Cinnamon Rolls

2 tortillas

2 Tbs. margarine

½ cup brown sugar

1 Tbs. cinnamon

¼ cup chopped nuts

1 Tbs. olive oil

Spread margarine on tortilla and sprinkle on brown sugar, cinnamon and chopped nuts. Roll up the tortilla and fry in olive oil in a covered pan.

Rice Pudding

1½ cup Minute Rice

¼ cup raisins

3 Tbs. brown sugar

¼ tsp. cinnamon

dash of nutmeg

¼ cup powdered milk

1 Tbs. powdered egg

1½ tsp flour

2 Tbs. jam

Combine first six ingredients and cook in 1 cup boiling water for 5 minutes. Mix powdered egg and flour together with enough water to make a paste, and add to rice mixture, stirring well. Top servings with jam.

Apple Crisp

Filling:

1½ cups dried apples, chopped

½ tsp. cinnamon or apple pie spice mix

hot water to just cover fruit in pot

½ cup chopped walnuts or almonds

½ cup raisins

¼ tsp. salt (optional)

Topping:

¼–½ cup oatmeal

3 Tbs. flour

4 heaping Tbs. margarine

3 Tbs. brown sugar

pinch of salt (optional)

Combine all filling ingredients except nuts in a pot and let soak until fruit rehydrates — about 15 minutes. Meanwhile combine the topping ingredients. Mix together with hands to a crumbly consistency. Grease a frypan. Add nuts to fruit mixture and pour into pan. (If there is a lot of liquid, stir in 1 Tbs. flour.) Cover with oatmeal mix. Bake, using a twiggy fire, for about 15 minutes until heated through and browned on top.

Basic Bannock

½ cup white flour

½ cup whole wheat flour

1 tsp. baking powder

3 Tbs. powdered milk

½ tsp. salt

Mix all dry ingredients and add water slowly until dough is slightly sticky. Separate into three to four patties and fry in an oiled frying pan over moderate heat until both sides are a golden brown.

Cajun Bannock

½ cup white flour

½ cup whole wheat flour

1 tsp. baking powder

3 Tbs. powdered milk

½ tsp. salt

pinch of garlic powder

pinch of onion powder

pinch of white pepper

pinch of cracked black pepper

pinch of cayenne pepper

pinch of dried thyme

pinch of dried oregano

1 Tbs. unsalted sunflower seeds

1 Tbs. olive oil

¼ cup water

Mix all dry ingredients and add water slowly until dough is slightly sticky. Separate into three to four patties and fry in an oiled frying pan over moderate heat until both sides are a golden brown.

Mark Robbins fries up a mess of pan-sized brook trout right on the portage.

My Super Pancakes

½ cup white flour

½ cup whole wheat flour

1 Tbs. powdered eggs

1 Tbs. powdered milk

½ tsp. baking powder

pinch of salt

1 tsp. cinnamon

¼ cup of dried cranberries

1 Tbs. olive oil

¼ cup water

Mix dry ingredients. Add water slowly to make batter. Fry in oiled pan at moderate heat. Serve with syrup.

Wild Nutrition

Instead of sipping on a cup of regular Earl Grey, why not steep a few pine needles or other types of foliage (spruce, cedar, wintergreen, wild strawberry, yellow birch twigs) to prepare a somewhat adequate, if not more flavorful cup of tea. Simply grab a handful or two of needles, twigs, or leaves and let them steep in boiling water for 5 to 7 minutes. Extra ingredients that I find add a little zest are a spoonful of brown sugar and a shot of liqueur.

True Grit Camp Coffee

True camp coffee is nothing but real grounds-and-water-in-the-pot coffee. Bring water to a rolling boil, take it off the heat source, dump in one generous tablespoon full of coffee grounds per cup of water, and let it steep (covered) alongside the campfire for approximately 5 to 10 minutes. To settle the grounds, tap a spoon on the side of the pot three to five times.

The most crucial element of brewing "true grit" is to never let the coffee boil once you've taken it off the heat source. Old-timers used to say that boiled coffee tastes like rotten shoe leather, and they're right! The reason for the bad taste of boiled coffee is in the bitter tannic acid and flavoring oils it contains. The tasty oils are released at 205 degrees Fahrenheit (86°C), just below boiling point. The bitter acids, however, are released right at or just above boiling pot.

Another important factor is how to settle the grounds before serving the coffee. Some people throw in pieces of eggshell or toss in a few round pebbles. I've even witnessed campers take hold of the wire handle on the pot, swing it with the speed of an aircraft propeller, and have complete faith in centrifugal force. This suicidal action will pull the grounds to the bottom of the pot — guaranteed. I merely tap the side of the pot with a knife or spoon and then make sure to offer the first and last cup of coffee to someone else in the group.

Bibliography

Armitage, Andrew. *The Sweetwater Explorer: Paddling in Grey and Bruce Counties.* Owen Sound: The Ginger Press, 1995.

Carpenter, Donna. *A Campers Guide to Ontario's Best Parks.* Erin, Ontario: The Boston Mills Press, 2000.

Chant, Edna B. *Beautiful Charleston.* Belleville, Ontario: Mika Publishing Company, 1975.

Dawber, Michael. *Where the Heck is Boleheck?: Unusual Place-Names From Eastern Ontario.* Burnstown, Ontario: The General Store Publishing House, 1995.

Fox, Sherwood. *The Bruce Beckons.* Toronto: University of Toronto Press, 1952.

Geddes, Hilda. *The Canadian Mississippi River.* Burnstown, Ontario: General Store Publishing House, 1988.

Grand River Conservation Authority. *Canoeing the Grand River: A Canoeing Guide to Ontario's Historic River.* Cambridge, Ontario: Grand River Conservation Authority, 1982.

Marleau, Jason, Russell Mussio and Wesley Mussio. *Mussio Adventures Presents Backroad Maps: Cottage Country Region.* New Westminister, B.C.: Mussio Adventures Ltd., 1999.

Ministry of Natural Resources, Minden District. *Poker Lake System Canoe Route* pamphlet.

Ministry of Natural Resources, Parks and Recreational Areas Branch, in cooperation with McClelland & Stewart. *Canoe Routes of Ontario.* Toronto: 1981.

Ministry of Natural Resources in cooperation with Friends of Bon Echo Park. *Kishkebus Canoe Trail* pamphlet. 1993

Ministry of Natural Resources. *Bon Echo Provincial Park Management Plan.* 1991

Ministry of Natural Resources. *Charleston Lake Provincial Park Management Plan.* 1991

Raffan, James, and Bert Horwood. *Canexus: The Canoe in Canadian Culture.* Toronto: Betelgeuse Books & Queen's University, 1988.

Reid, Ron, and Janet Grand. *Canoeing Ontario's Rivers.* Vancouver/Toronto: Douglas & McIntyre, 1985.

Taim, Astrid. *Almagun: A Highland History.* Toronto: Natural Heritage/Natural History Inc., 1998.

The Upper Thames Conservation Authority. *The Upper Thames Canoe Route: St. Marys to Delaware* pamphlet.

Zyvatkauskas, Betty. *Naturally Ontario: Exploring the Wealth of Ontario's Wild Places.* Toronto: Random House of Canada, 1999.

Web Resources

www.100-acrewood.virtualave.net/quotes/quotes.htm "Christopher Robin Quotes."

www.disney.go.com/DisneyRecords/read-alongs/Pooh "Walt Disney Records: Winnie the Pooh & the Blustery Day Read-Along."

www.geocities.com/EnchantedForest/3278/wtp/pooh-transcript.htm "The Many Adventures of Winnie the Pooh."

www.interlog.com/erhard/1989pruling.htm "Portage Ruling — Credit River, Ontario."

www.just-pooh.com/history.html "Winnie the Pooh — History of Pooh."

www.mazinaw.on.ca "Friends of Bon Echo Home Page."

www.ontarioparks.com "Ontario Parks."

www.thamesriver.org "Upper Thames Conservation Authority."

www.sentex.net "Rockwood, Now This Is Heaven."

www.waynecook.com/asimcoe.html "Historical Plaques of Ontario."

www.webpan.com/canoetoutes/FS-Resources.htm "Ontario Canoe Routes."